I AM BECOMING!

Dwayne A. Walker

Note: The names satan, enemy, accuser, opposition, and other references to the devil are capitalized not to show respect. It is simply to adhere to English capitalization rules.

ISBN: 978-1-7359790-0-7

DEDICATION

This book is dedicated to every person who has attempted to apply the principles of the best-selling book of all time, the Bible, to their daily lives, but has failed to do so consistently. It's for individuals who are determined to overcome their problems, seize opportunities, and no longer want to be negatively influenced by the voices that try to limit their potential. May you realize that God is constantly working to help you fulfill your purpose, regardless of the obstacles, shortcomings, or accomplishments you're currently experiencing.

The LORD will work out his plans for my life—for your faithful love,
O LORD endures forever. Don't abandon me, for you made me.
— Psalm 138:8 NLT

ACKNOWLEDGMENTS

None of us ever truly "arrive." Instead, we are constantly maturing, growing, and being molded by what we focus on, our experiences, and our relationships. I'm so thankful to everyone who is helping to shape me.

I'm thankful for my slice of heaven on Earth, my family—My wife Mogda, who continually gives me unconditional love, support, and inspiration, and my children Nicholas, Amaris, Christopher, and my grandchildren, Trey, Kai, and Dreux, who continue to amaze me and fill my life with so much joy and laughter. I am profoundly and forever grateful to God for blessing me with such an incredible family.

I'm particularly thankful to my mother, whom I call my "Doctor of Inspiration," because of her regular spiritual advice and motivation. Her calls, saying, "I heard a good one this morning," referring to a sermon from her church or one she saw on television, are almost always perfectly timed. Mom, I can't express my appreciation enough for your words of support, guidance, care, love, and faith in me.

I sincerely thank Pastor Brooks and all the selfless morning prayer warriors at Stones Church. You were invaluable in helping to provide me with a rich vocabulary, patterns, and consistency of prayer. When you launched the Daily Online Prayer, it helped me build a stronger spiritual foundation and experience prayer's power and positive results in my life.

I am immensely thankful to my cornermen—Nate, Marco, and Alan—for motivating and pushing me to finish this book. Thanks, Charlie Sander—your encouragement, feedback on the proofs, and insightful editing suggestions were incredibly beneficial! You helped create a much better final manuscript.

Additionally, I want to thank my personally-chosen digital mentors, who have invaluably touched my life—Og Mandino and the late, great leader and visionary Dr. Myles Munroe.

I appreciate the PUREFLIX streaming service team for successfully executing their mission of offering faith-based and family-friendly content that *transforms lives, inspires hearts, and lifts the spirits of their subscribers.* I have lost count of the times when their service has provided me with the precise motivational, humorous, yet faith-centered "mini-inspirational boost" I needed.

To Freda, our first customer at ChicagoLand Popcorn, a trusted confidant, an appreciated prayer intercessor, and my "sister from another mother," who shares the same Father, our Heavenly Father. It's amazing how your simple act of obedience to give me a "momma" hug brought me such a dear and trusted friend.

To my readers, thank you for allowing me to share how I've used the Word to shape my life. His Word works and does not come back void (Isaiah 55:8-11), so as you meditate on it, expect change!

And last, but certainly not least, thanks to my big brother, my Lord, and Savior, Jesus Christ (Hebrews 2:11-12). Because You did, I can. Thank you!

> *Don't judge each day by the harvest you reap,*
> *but by the seeds that you plant.*
> —ROBERT LOUIS STEVENSON

ABOUT THE COVER

Stop staring at the mountains. Climb them instead! Yes, it's a harder process, but it will lead you to a better view.
— ANONYMOUS

The cover photo shows two climbers. One is on the side of the peak, working to achieve his goal, while the other is standing at the top, taking a moment to celebrate her hard work and achievement.

Mountain climbing techniques illustrate an excellent example of how we approach and conquer the peaks we face in life. Rarely does a climber ascend a mountain by going straight up. With specialized equipment, a zigzag pattern is used to go up and around obstacles and leverage more accessible routes. Additionally, less force is required to ascend when one reduces the Earth's gravitational pull by using short, lateral moves to climb.

Like climbing physical peaks, the deliberate and focused application of God's Word helps us overcome obstacles and challenges with small, often overlooked victories and daily progress.

Mountaineers often miss the view and majestic beauty of the climb because they must remain focused to avoid hazards.

However, even seemingly insignificant accomplishments can be acknowledged, celebrated, and amplified daily, profoundly impacting our self-worth and motivation.

Finally, both climbing and life require setting goals with deadlines and planning, as if one's life depends on them because it does. We can't scale any mountains until we begin to climb. So let's get started today and make I AM BECOMING! your daily mantra!

THE I AM BECOMING! MISSION

To help people discover, awaken,
and utilize their talents and gifts to fulfill their purpose.

We are searching worldwide with great enthusiasm for people and groups to whom we can bring the I AM BECOMING! Mission.

Our goal is to help millions realize that *the harvest of accomplishment lies not in good intentions but in purposefully sowing to release the latent potential of everyday life.*

We encourage people from all walks of life to realize that everything they need to reach their destiny was given to them at birth! Simply put, we help people and organizations to *transform potential into purpose*!

A percentage of the royalties from each copy of I AM BECOMING! is donated to chosen non-profit charities and ministries, which also assist people in uncovering, activating, and using their talents and gifts to fulfill their purpose.

Thanks for helping us help others!

The road to failure is paved with bricks of good intentions — the
vehicle used to travel it is powered by idleness. ACT NOW!
— DWAYNE A. WALKER

To order bulk copies, discuss speaking engagements or consulting programs,
please visit dwayneAwalker.com/inquiries

A NOTE TO YOU

For years, I had heard about the power and truth of the Bible. I grew up attending church and hearing stories of God's grace and salvation through His Son, Jesus. But despite all my familiarity with the Bible, I struggled to read and understand how to apply it to the different areas of my life. It wasn't just difficult—it was so challenging that it often caused me to feel discouraged, even before I started reading!

I tried all sorts of things—reading different translations, studying select topics alone or with Bible study groups, and listening to a library of sermons—but I lacked a way to help me consistently apply it to everyday challenges. Despite my best efforts, my lack of progress often left me feeling defeated and disheartened. I knew something had to change, but I wasn't sure where to turn.

Years passed, and I settled into a comfortable routine of attending church on Sundays and nodding in agreement with the pastor's comments. But deep down, I still longed to understand and connect the Bible and the God who wrote it to the issues I would face every Monday morning!

One day I realized that I was focusing much of my prayer time on articulating my problems instead of seeking and speaking biblically-inspired solutions! Then, I recalled a story that my pastor from the church I attended when I lived in Michigan said about me during a sermon. He recounted a dream he once had where I was holding a Bible and standing in front of sheets of 8.5 x 11-inch paper taped on the wall. My problems were written on them. Each time I looked at an issue, I found a scripture that provided an answer. I would then raise my Bible like a hammer and swing it down toward the problem while speaking its biblical solution. BAM! I answered the issue with the power of the Word.

I'd tried everything before, but remembering my pastor's dream caught my attention. I began to read the Bible more meaningfully and to look for practical solutions to problems.

As I started working on declarations, I decided to include some problems my family and friends faced. The short, Word-packed declarations were unlike anything I'd tried before, and they helped me connect with God in a way I never had.

As I created more declarations, I began seeing the Bible in a new light. The stories that had once seemed dry and confusing now came alive with meaning and relevance. I asked questions, took more notes, and started sharing my declarations via social media and email.

Today, I still don't have all the answers. Some parts of the Bible continue to challenge me, but thanks to the I AM BECOMING! Program, I have renewed confidence and curiosity regarding the

Bible. I know there's always more to discover, more to learn, and more to explore. So, I'll keep reading, keep searching, and keep uncovering.

TRUE IDENTITY

People have become fascinated with discovering their identities through various means, like personality assessments, quizzes, and tests. The internet is full of websites, videos, and blogs that offer options to help find answers. However, as for the Bible, people are created in God's image and are called and given the freedom to find their identity in Him. While I AM BECOMING! is not a "religious" text, I have included some of my core beliefs as a person of faith in this book. These principles have been instrumental in helping me discover who I am.

Understanding our authority and identity in Jesus Christ, as defined in the Bible, reveals who we truly are. Our relationship with Him determines our identity in Him. Education, social status, job title, or wealth does not define it. Knowing God intimately is what leads to great accomplishments!

Many people allow their identities, dreams, and goals to get buried under hurts, disappointments, or shaped by past failures. Others live with the nagging thought of regret—"I wish I *would* have, *could* have, or *should* have done this or that."

SUCCESS

Surprisingly, the obstacles that stop us are often due to something other than significant problems or big failures. Instead, they result from an accumulation of little thoughts which impact our daily steps toward a desired future. The Opposition may not even have to attempt to limit some people. They decide not to try to seek their goals anymore. Proverbs 23:7 states, *"For as he thinketh in his heart, so is he."*

My late friend, the great Muhammad Ali, once said, "The fight is won or lost far away from the witnesses, behind the lines, in the gym, and out there on the road, long before I dance under those lights." The hourly, daily, and weekly decisions to keep pursuing his dreams held the key to his success.

In his audio program "Lead the Field," Earl Nightingale defines success this way: "Success is the progressive realization of a worthy goal."

Both Muhammad Ali and Earl Nightingale reiterated that success is characterized not just by reaching one's ultimate goal, but also by the transformational journey one takes to get there. The untold and what some might consider the mundane, repetitive, and unseen story behind the lights contains the key. The mindset and thoughts which carry us during behind-the-scenes activities and progress hold *the true secrets to achievement.*

I've observed three responses to the pressures and trials of life that hinder momentum. Some people do nothing and silently suffer; some try to find things to take away the pain of the effort to progress or to get over past failures; and finally, many seek God for help to find solutions. However, the thoughts and feelings that follow disappointment, unfulfillment, and regret keep most people from progressing. The Enemy wants you to believe you have missed your opportunity to fulfill your purpose.

The truth is, nothing that happens in our lives surprises God. He's already seen and knows everything; the good and the bad, the favor and the setbacks. (Psalm 139:16-18 NLT) Regardless of the cause, God has already orchestrated a path back to your destiny! The challenge is that our thinking, beliefs, and confessions limit what He can do to help us!

Matthew 13:53-58 states, "Jesus did only a few miracles because of their unbelief." It did not read that He "couldn't do miracles," but that He "did only a few miracles." It appears as if Jesus didn't have a choice in the matter. This is stunning! Unbelief prevents the power of God from moving in our lives! Belief and unbelief are both tremendous spiritual forces and are the fuels that drive our actions. We are either driven by belief (faith) or hindered by unbelief (misapplied faith, doubt). There is no neutral ground. Faith is *always* at work!

Progress in life is much like the climbers scaling the mountain on the cover of this book. We ascend as long as we hang on and climb. If we let go or stop, like gravity, the opposing forces of life halt or erase our advancement.

My life as an entrepreneur, author, and keynote speaker, focuses on helping people acknowledge who they are and also helping them accelerate daily progress toward their purposes and destinies. I'm committed to helping people to see themselves, and others, as God does. I have no hesitation in saying, "I AM BECOMING!" is one of the most valuable and practical methods of applying the Word of God to support a change in thinking. How you achieve is determined by the thoughts you believe, recall, and rehearse.

I'm honored to share some of my personal study notes and declarations on the following pages. I've worked tirelessly to ensure this book becomes an invaluable "life-progressing" tool worthy of your time, focus, and application. Thank you for allowing me to become part of your journey and life!

Keep Becoming!

DAW

You may not control all the events that happen to you,
but you can decide not to be reduced by them.
— MAYA ANGELOU

Be yourself; everyone else is already taken.
— OSCAR WILDE

CONTENTS

INTRODUCTION

*Owning our story and loving ourselves through that process
is the bravest thing that we will ever do.*
—BRENE' BROWN

TAKE RESPONSIBILITY

Early in my senior year of high school, thanks to my father, one of my heroes, I refocused my attention to better understand the mountain we all have to climb—called *Life*.

THE GARAGE TALK

"Dwayne, come to the garage with me for a minute." I was unsure why my father had asked me to follow him. Surely, we wouldn't start a new car repair or undertake any other projects this late in the evening. It was past 8:00 pm, and I had just arrived home from my part-time after-school job.

1

"Dwayne, I want you to know I'm proud of you," my dad stated as he turned and held a relaxed, unnerving gaze into my eyes while reaching out to shake my hand.

"Thanks, Pops," I said, still unsure of why he called me into the garage.

"Dwayne, I'm very proud of you," he repeated. "You're becoming an independent young man, and I just wanted you to know that I recognize that fact." He continued, "You're working a part-time job and making a few dollars." "You've even saved and bought your own transportation." (I had purchased a small motorcycle during the summer of my sophomore year.) "You're picking out and buying some of your school clothes, can pretty much go where you want, and eat what you like to eat." He paused, then flashed his trademark sheepish smile just as I started standing a little taller and sticking out my chest in appreciation of my dad's compliments.

He continued, "Dwayne, I don't want to mess up your newfound independence." He paused again, "I don't want you to become an *independent*-dependent." As he continued, I raised my eyebrows and looked at him confusedly. He then proceeded to answer questions I hadn't asked. "You see, son, you live in my house and sleep in a bed I provide. You primarily eat my food, and even though you have a little motorcycle, you frequently drive a vehicle I provide. Finally, I pay for the bulk of your clothes."

2

Where was Pops going with these comments? Little did I know how skillfully he was getting to his point.

"Dwayne, I've noticed you haven't applied to any colleges or trade schools, so I want to clarify your post-graduation options long before the end of your senior year."

He held up one finger. "Your first option is that you can go directly to college, like your brother, or get into a trade school." "If you choose either option, you can come home during holiday and summer breaks."

Then he held up two fingers to indicate his second point. "Your next option is to go into the military as I did. (My father was a veteran of the U.S. Air Force.) If you follow this path, you can come home during scheduled leaves."

Holding up three fingers, he made his third and what I thought was his final point. "If you don't want to pursue these options, you're welcome to live at home with us."

As I stared at him with a puzzled look, he continued as he grinned again. Shrugging his shoulders and tilting his head slightly to one side, he made his fourth point, "But if you choose to stay home, I'm going to have to charge you rent—and it won't be cheap."

What happened? What did my father just say? His attempt to prevent me from becoming an *independent*-dependent felt like he was putting me out!

I immediately began to reflect on the lessons and experiences of my past, as my father had desired. I suddenly became consumed with thinking about my future. I was already scaling the mountain called *Life*, even though it felt as if I had just been pushed off one of the peaks. Thank God for my father and his unique method of getting my attention.

> *Life is not a problem to be solved, but a reality to be experienced.*
> —SOREN KIERKEGAARD

A SECOND CHANCE

High school is supposed to be a stepping-stone for young people to lay a firm foundation and prepare for a career and a fulfilling life. Students are encouraged to develop critical thinking skills, engage in spirited conversations, pursue their passions, and advance academically to open themselves to a lifetime of learning. During my four years of high school, I developed another interesting talent—I became an expert at concealment.

I'd struggled so much through my early years that I had very poor self-esteem when I entered high school. Most people who met and got to know me found me likable, but I never felt I truly fit in. I was a 5'6", skinny, 135-pound kid with average coordination, below-average athletic ability, and 1/4-inch-thick glasses resting on my boyish face.

My first date was the senior prom, and I went into it knowing I was the second, third, or even lower-choice option for my date. Needless to say, I wasn't the most popular guy in school.

The only classes I excelled in were Band, Shop, and Introduction to Computer Programming. I graduated with an overall GPA of 2.5. I scored just well enough on my SAT to get accepted into only one college. Even there, my admission was conditional until I completed a unique program called the Martin Luther King (MLK) Student Program. This was my *second chance*!

The MLK program was developed to service socio-economically disadvantaged minority students who lacked traditional university entrance qualifications. It was an intense six-week structured summer indoctrination into college life before the Fall semester. We went through a specially-tailored curriculum, which included reading, writing, and developing study habits, along with an introduction to dorm living. For the first time in my academic experience, I learned *how* to study and overcome several of my many bad habits.

FOCUS

After being compelled to embrace the responsibility of taking control of my life, things improved in many areas once I moved onto campus. I started actively focusing on and chasing the dreams that I finally began to believe were possible.

To the surprise of many, in my first semester, I got a part-time work-study position as a Computer Programmer for a professor in the Chemistry Department. In my sophomore year, I added a second job as an Input/Output Operator in the computer lab a few nights a week. That same year, I eliminated my room and board expenses by earning a coveted Resident Advisor position in my dormitory. The summer before my junior year, an internship at the Kellogg Company gave me valuable experience and enabled me to afford my first off-campus apartment. I held the position as a permanent, part-time Programmer until I graduated two years later with a B.S. in Computer Science and a Minor in Applied Mathematics.

When I returned for my high school class reunion, I received an award for being the "Most-Changed" class member. Not only had I attended and finished college, which shocked almost everyone, but I had also grown six inches and put on over forty pounds!

Despite my dramatic physical changes and academic success, I had not improved my self-esteem. While I began to experience limited outward progress, I was not doing what I needed to do to grow my inner man—the real me.

One big reason for this was that, even though I'd discovered who I was, I still thought I had to fix my shortcomings before embracing my future. I repeatedly spent so much time looking backward that I prevented my forward progress!

I thought that if I continued to embrace and run after a more clearly defined destiny, I'd automatically start to distance myself from the many things clouding my judgment, creating "noise," and holding me back. Unfortunately, this was not the case. Thankfully, I eventually began to understand that I needed to *know the real me* — to *reveal the real me*.

THE LIFE-JOURNEY CONTINUES

Years later, in dismay, I put my hands over my head as I attempted to make sense of my life. The financial pressures I faced then were, at times, suffocating.

Almost a decade had passed since I'd turned down a position that would have required a move to another state. I'd decided not to allow my vocation to determine my location. Instead, I'd chosen to leave a lucrative senior executive career and became a full-time entrepreneur! I was convinced this change would accelerate my progress toward my destiny.

I had dreams and set goals, but when "life happened," it surprised me how easy it was to get lost, chasing the things I thought I wanted. I struggled to recognize and accept my path. Inconsistent progress became sobering.

Becoming an entrepreneur gave me the independence to define and express myself freely. However, it also began to amplify my shortcomings—which the culture of a large corporate environment had enabled me to hide from myself and others!

Peering into the mirror during my morning shaves, I often felt I didn't know the guy trapped in that reflection. How had my desire to pursue my goals caused my current circumstances? How and why had my decisions led me here?

Many of us spend our lives working to achieve success or gain the approval "they" said we should have. We spend so much time trying to be something other than who we are. Yet, deep down, we remember our true selves! The impressions of others shouldn't define who we are. Our hidden feelings and character, not our reputations, define us.

I know I know—who doesn't experience challenges at some point? Encountering challenges is typical, but developing and staying in a frustrating, unfulfilled lifestyle is, unfortunately, where many of us live.

How we achieve is determined by the story of our lives, which we conceive, believe, and rehearse in our minds. How do we create a positive outline for our stories? How do we recognize and trust that the things we're going through are a part of the process? Do you believe nothing surprises God in your past, present, or future?

My hidden belief of being hindered and helpless to change, resulted in my failing to fully embrace my journey and develop a hopeful vision for my future. I wanted to create a path based on what God says about me in His Word. But I'd become indifferent to so many things I was unable to recognize and acknowledge even small daily accomplishments! I slowly slipped into a quiet state of continual conformity.

Are we missing out on God's best because we don't realize everything we need to enhance our journey has already been provided? Many are living below the level of provision God desires for us. We should all become more conscious of how much time we waste trying to provide solutions to problems that have already been solved!

If you've encountered significant life-obstacles or endured substantial setbacks, remember that *these challenges don't define who you are!* Just because things are not going as planned doesn't mean they'll stay that way! Nor do they indicate you're not making progress. You don't know your entire story! Don't get lost in the temporary circumstances you discover on your climb. Sometimes, we become so conscious of what we *don't have*—we overlook what we *already possess!*

IF YOU ONLY CONCENTRATE ON WHAT YOU *DON'T* HAVE, YOU'LL OFTEN OVERLOOK WHAT YOU *DO* HAVE!

Subsequently, while we remain hopeful about our faith, we commonly lack the enthusiasm to share our beliefs and confidently encourage others. We often feel our lives would offer little motivation to non-believers, especially if we face the same issues they do, year after year!

Praying and declaring God's Word profoundly impacts our relationship and trust in Him. Rather than relying on our abilities, we acknowledge that God is the One who can change our circumstances and guide us toward our purpose.

Even if our current position in life is not what we desire, we can take comfort in knowing that God has already equipped us for our intended purposes. We can find peace and confidence during difficult situations by trusting Him and seeking His guidance.

Prayer and the declaration of God's Word remind us of His sovereignty over our lives. By submitting to His will and trusting in His plans, we can find the strength and courage to navigate the ups and downs of life with grace and resilience.

The "I AM BECOMING!" declarations (prayers) are designed to give a quick, targeted infusion of the Word to help quiet the noise of life. This book provides just one way to creatively attain Bible-based inspiration in a relevant and consistent manner.

Don't just talk with your lips as you read and speak the declarations. Open your heart to God, and He will hear you. God speaks heart language!

The I AM BECOMING! Program is not intended to answer every question or give solutions to every problem, but if followed, you'll begin to work the Word into your life. I encourage you to see how your faith can inspire others as you experience recognizable progress. Use what you have right where you are. I AM BECOMING! I encourage you to BECOME, too!

Hebrews 12:1 NLT

Therefore, since we are surrounded by such a huge crowd of witnesses to the life of faith, let us strip off every weight that slows us down, especially the sin that so easily trips us up. And let us run with endurance, the race God has set before us.

The two most important days in your life,
are the day you are born, and the day you find out why.
—MARK TWAIN

PART 1

–1–

KNOW WHO YOU ARE

You are not a human being in search of a spiritual experience.
You are a spiritual being immersed in a human experience.
— PIERRE TEILHARD DE CHARDIN

Many individuals find it challenging to progress in their lives because they've fallen into the trap of wrongly imagining how others perceive them. This mindset leads to a persistent negative self-image. This common tactic and deception of the Enemy, as referenced in Numbers 13:33, is widespread in many societal groups. It restricts millions from experiencing a better quality of life and hope for advancement.

Pride, fear, and the condemning voice of the Accuser, due to prior missteps, cause many to hide their perceived or actual inadequacies. Instead of investing time and energy in discovering their true identity, as the Bible describes, the emphasis becomes the creative art of concealment. God is aware of the lies that prevent us from seeing ourselves the way He does. He knows the flawed way we see ourselves. If we're going to be restored and fulfill our destiny, we must be open and honest with ourselves and God. He's capable and willing to help us change, but it's not up to God alone. It's up to us, too! Knowing and accepting the granted authority in God's creative process gives us the ability and freedom to change our living conditions.

Discovering who we are begins by asking God for forgiveness and accepting Jesus Christ as our savior. When we sincerely do this, He forgives us! Our actions may have consequences, but we're FREE to move forward from past mistakes!

Come along with me during the remainder of this chapter as I summarize the power and authority given to man by God. I encourage you to read and meditate on the referenced scriptures, as they will feed your faith and give you a firm foundation upon which to build. If you'd like to establish or renew your relationship with God, please visit the Appendix for the next steps.

GOVERNMENT

A government has been defined as a group of people who have the ability to rule within a defined territory. Today's five primary forms of worldly powers are democracy, oligarchy, aristocracy, dictatorship, and monarchy, with a king or queen.

While I support the government and other organizations to provide leadership and create laws, each person is responsible for governing him or herself. Romans 13:1 states that God has supreme authority and dominion over everything.

Romans 13:1 [NLT]
Everyone must submit to governing authorities. For all authority comes from God, and those in positions of authority have been placed there by God.

People, organizations, political parties, and other leadership groups often claim their guiding beliefs are founded on biblical principles. Tragically, many who embrace these movements, including professed believers, seem to understand little about the Kingdom of God's priorities and the position and rights granted to its citizens. They put unprecedented desire and trust into man-made government policies instead of being *agents of change*, using their God-given supernatural authority to shape their worlds positively.

KINGDOM OF HEAVEN

The Kingdom of Heaven, also called the Kingdom of God, is the unseen spiritual realm over which God reigns as King. Several scriptures reveal that God has absolute rule over this realm, including all tangible creations.

Daniel 4:3

How great are his signs! and how mighty are his wonders! his kingdom is an everlasting kingdom, and his dominion is from generation to generation.

Psalm 103:19

The LORD hath prepared his throne in the heavens; and his kingdom ruleth over all.

John 1:3

All things were made by him; and without him was not anything made that was made.

The Kingdom of Heaven is the rule by an eternal, sovereign God over everything seen and unseen. The first principle to understand is that God has supreme authority over *all* earthly governments.

GOD HAS SUPREME AUTHORITY OVER *ALL* EARTHLY GOVERNMENTS

DOMINION

The word dominion means to be in charge of or rule over. God spoke, and His Words formed every detail of this world and created a physical domain. The completion represented the fulfillment of His will on Earth.

God created man, male and female, in His image, as His crowning creation. He gave them dominion and rule over the realm explicitly designed for them. Thus, the human race became Kingdom Agents, appointed as the world's rulers. God gave us everything and put it under our control to be dominated by us.

Genesis 1:26-28

And God said, "Let us make man in our image, after our likeness: and let them have dominion over the fish of the sea, and over the fowl of the air, and over the cattle, and over all the earth, and over every creeping thing that creepeth upon the earth." [27] So God created man in his own image, in the image of God created he him; male and female created he them. [28] And God blessed them, and God said unto them, "Be fruitful, and multiply, and replenish the earth, and subdue it: and have dominion over the fish of the sea, and over the fowl of the air, and over every living thing that moveth upon the earth."

As quoted earlier, the second principle is to realize that we are not human beings searching for a spiritual experience—we are spiritual beings immersed in a human physical experience.

Discovering the laws and rules governing our immersion helps us define who we are and allows us to maximize our potential.

WE ARE SPIRITUAL BEINGS, GRANTED DOMINION OVER AND IMMERSED INTO A HUMAN PHYSICAL EXPERIENCE

MULTIPLY

Although God performed the original creation, He wanted man to become a co-laborer with Him and to learn to walk in the dominion he had been granted. So God gave Adam the first known internship to help awaken and develop his creative ability. God created by speaking. He allowed Adam to speak and gave him authority to name every living creature.

Genesis 2:19-20

And out of the ground the LORD God formed every beast of the field, and every fowl of the air; and brought them unto Adam to see what he would call them: and whatsoever Adam called every living creature, that was the name thereof. [20] And Adam gave names to all cattle, and to the fowl of the air, and to every beast of the field; but for Adam there was not found an help meet for him. [21] So the LORD God caused the man to fall into a deep sleep. While the man slept, the LORD God took out one of the man's ribs and closed up the opening. [22] Then the LORD God made a woman from the rib, and he brought her to the man. [23] At last! the man exclaimed. This one is bone from my bone, and flesh from my flesh! She will be called 'woman,' because she was taken from 'man.'

God knew Adam needed a companion, so he formed a co-creator to work with him. Adam called her woman and later named her Eve because she would become the mother of all who lived. (Genesis 3:20 NLT) Eve was created Adam's equal, spiritually, intellectually, and morally. They were empowered to be fruitful and multiply, to answer God's command. They were responsible for filling the Earth with their productions and themselves. *Together* they would bring new life into the world — something neither could do independently.

They were to sow the seeds of their talents and gifts into the Earth's womb and be productive using the planet's resources. To reproduce himself, Adam, who had seed, was required to join Eve, who had a womb, and thus as directed, multiply and increase the number of people on Earth.

WE ARE CO-LABORERS IN THE CREATION PROCESS AND ARE ALLOWED TO IMAGINE, GIVE IDENTITY TO, MULTIPLY, AND EXPERIENCE FRUITFULNESS AND SUCCESS

MAN'S FALL

The loss of man's granted authority came in Genesis, Chapter 3, which described man's sin, and subsequent fall from his dominion position. Since then, all have been born into this fallen state. However, God did not abandon His desire and purpose for creating man. He immediately put His *Plan For Redemption* into motion.

WHO WE ARE

The central theme of the Bible is how the Kingdom of God is established on Earth. It describes the works of creation, how man was given provision and granted dominion over it, judgment, and how man lost sovereignty; but regained standing through salvation! God then lays out man's priorities to once again live in the authority He bestowed upon him. The Bible's divinely inspired pages lead us to the door of our redemption — the Death, Burial, and Resurrection of Jesus.

THE CHOICE

Before birth, God puts everything in us that we need to reach our full potential. His unconditional love is not dependent on who we are or what we've done. He allows us the freedom to choose to love Him back as we work to achieve our goals. We openly deny Him by not seeking a daily relationship with Him. We should be discovering, developing, and sowing the talents and gifts granted to us to exercise dominion and multiply. He wants to help us — if we would only sincerely ask!

Some may think it's too late to achieve their dreams and desires or reach their imagined destiny. If you are 40, 50, 60, 70, or even older — if God woke you up this morning, it means He's not finished developing you! You have another opportunity to grow and Become! Your years of experience have shown you what works and what doesn't. Your time and efforts were well spent— if you've learned. Use failure as fuel to progress. NEVER STOP BELIEVING! God didn't give the promise and potential to live a fulfilled life, a gender, race, education restriction, or expiration date!

Jesus is the door to our redemption. However, God made man's mind the doorkeeper to bring an unseen kingdom reality into our daily relationships, opportunities, and challenges. God does not *need us* to make things happen. *He allows* us to be His change agents, and active participants, in creating our desired lives.

THE HABIT OF FAILURE

It's frustrating to have a vision for our future but habitually limit our efforts by thinking incorrectly about our qualifications and abilities.

Many enter into relationships, go to school, work, or engage in other activities desiring positive results, yet subconsciously not fully expecting to achieve anything! Think of the struggle: Going to work every day to earn money but always expecting to remain broke, or going to a doctor to get help for an illness but not fully believing you'll get well! This kind of thinking can become a living hell; unfortunately, it is where many people live. What essentially happens is that the Enemy of our souls hijacks the dominion authority and creative power God has granted to man.

What you think about matters because it forms the basis of who you will become. Our thinking enables, or limits, our abilities to reach a desired future and walk with unwavering confidence, as His children and citizens of His Kingdom!

FROM HEARING TO DOING

We are Co-laborers. God gives us the privilege, as Kingdom citizens, to invite Him into our daily lives and situations to see them changed. How do we grow from just knowing principles to embracing and consistently using them? How do we develop, mature, and boldly learn to use our restored authority and dominion as believers? How do we become examples to share God's message of life, hope, and truth with the world? *The only way to* routinely walk consistently in dominion is to view ourselves and the world—from God's perspective.

Failed personal and business relationships and ventures, financial struggles, family tragedies, and other stress associated with

24

everyday life can sometimes make us think and believe we are being defeated. If not checked and replaced, these thoughts can lead us to speak and perform unproductive actions in areas where we once had hopes, desires, and even prior success!

In his book, *Rediscovering the Kingdom* (Expanded Edition), Myles Munroe stated, "We are not responsible for establishing policy; we are responsible only for carrying out the policies established by the King. It is not our job to decide what to believe and think. Our job is to learn and discern what our King thinks, and then come into agreement with Him."

The power of God's Word transforms our lives as we declare and speak it by faith into our hearts. Creation and change are progressive, and our mind's transformation will only come if we consistently and deliberately apply the Word. (Romans 12:2)

No matter your past experiences or current circumstances, you can chart a new path toward your desired destination! Even if you faced challenges, such as growing up in poverty, enduring severe abuse, or dealing with seemingly impossible debt, having a renewed mind is the key to achieving *lasting* transformation.

Instead of allowing negative thoughts to linger and doubts to persist, we should shift our focus to embracing the positive image

God has of us, and holding onto the promises and desires He's ordained for our lives. Doing so will help us overcome any obstacles, including doubt and discouragement, that may try to hold us back.

We are commissioned and equipped to walk in dominion, no matter where we are in life. We are encouraged to know who we are, approach every day faithfully, and live prosperously in every area of our lives!

Personal development books, motivational speeches, and encouraging videos may contribute to our progress. However, deep down, the core of who we are can only be shaped, molded, and renewed by the Word of God.

SEEKING GOD'S KINGDOM

When you understand seeking wholeheartedly, you shape and fill your schedule around Him, and won't just "work Him into your day," if you get time. Meditating on and reciting Word-packed declarations, followed by purposely slowing down to listen, will allow you to meet Him and get to know His voice.

Actively seeking doesn't mean that God's love is earned. God is with us, whether our thoughts and hearts are focused on Him or not. The big exception is that we begin to hear and see things we may not have previously recognized. We begin to notice who and where we are as we open the door to a more purposely transparent relationship with Him. As we calm the busyness of life and quiet our minds, He's there waiting for *each of us*.

Your best days are still ahead, and your contributions to this world will make a difference to others as you grow and become who you're called to be!

In the long run, we shape our lives, and we shape ourselves.
The process never ends until we die.
And the choices we make are ultimately our own responsibility.
— ELEANOR ROOSEVELT

–2–

KNOW WHERE YOU ARE

*Your present circumstances don't determine where you can go;
they merely determine where you start.*
—NIDO QUBEIN

We use maps for many different reasons, including to help us find the best route and calculate trip times. Maps also allow us to explore and determine future destination options.

Whether planning a trip or your life's journey, the first rule of map reading is to *know where you are.* Concerning your life's journey, the second rule is to accept your findings, understanding that you're right where you're supposed to be at this time—however, you don't have to stay there! Applying God's Word to help navigate our everyday experiences, feelings, and circumstances will ultimately lead us to a more satisfying life.

So many people go through life feeling as if they should be somewhere else, doing something else, and living differently than they are. I'm not talking about people with ambition, desires, and a yearning for growth and advancement. I'm referring to people who feel "wrong" about where they are and constantly criticize themselves. They habitually focus on their faults, weaknesses, and past decisions, which led them to their current circumstances.

Focusing on yesterday and being down on yourself for past decisions won't help you identify and embrace new directions. Thinking poorly about your current status doesn't help you achieve more. Constant negative thinking is the primary reason so many live unfulfilled lives.

SUFFERING THE CONSEQUENCES OF BAD DECISIONS DOESN'T MEAN YOU'RE CONDEMNED. GOD FORGIVES! PERIOD.

After reciting the prayer of salvation (see Appendix), many people fall into the trap of, "I have to fix this," "When I change that," and "Once I stop this." They believe God will only accept them and help them improve their lives after they get everything "right." This mindset is a favorite trick of the Enemy and a distraction that stops us before we start to make significant progress on our new life's journey!

You may be living with the consequences of bad decisions. You may feel locked up in your mind with negative thoughts about your future or actually be physically incarcerated. Wherever you are, the Accuser's voice will continually speak and attempt to diminish your sense of worth and security. In our never-ending self-talk conversations, he disguises his deceitful suggestions to sound like your voice

HOW TO START YOUR JOURNEY

The Word tells us that God has removed our sin from us, as far as the East is from the West. (Psalm 103:12) But we keep remembering, even though God forgives us and forgets! (Romans 4:4-8 NLT) This forgetfulness is one of the most misunderstood details of our relationship with God. Unlike people who may forgive you but never forget, when we sincerely go to God and ask for forgiveness, He forgives, puts it out of his mind, and forgets. He erases it from the pages of time as if it never happened! I began to understand the difference between salvation and the consequences of actions. This revelation transformed my thinking, expectations, and focus for my future.

How do we fully embrace our current circumstances, including our flaws, missed opportunities, and failures? How can we simultaneously feel optimistic about our future? The answers lie in acknowledging that God transforms us and takes us from one level of glory to another. He starts from right where we are.

31

2 Corinthians 3:18 NKJV

But we all, with unveiled face, beholding as in a mirror the glory of the Lord, are being transformed into the same image from glory to glory, just as by the Spirit of the Lord.

This passage reveals that God is aware that change is a process. You're not required to fix all your shortcomings and flaws before you qualify for help from God. He is the potter—we are the clay. (Isaiah 64:8) God knew us before we were born (Jeremiah 1:5). The process of becoming more and more like Him starts the instant we accept Him. It continues for the rest of our earthly lives.

"From glory to glory" does not mean you start at zero. It means you start from wherever you are. When you accept Christ, God wholly accepts *you* RIGHT WHERE YOU ARE! This unrestricted acceptance is sometimes difficult to receive. The Accuser wants you to believe you're not accepted, so you'll achieve less or not grow!

ESCAPE VELOCITY

There's a common thread among successful businesspeople, great parents, superstar athletes, award-winning entertainers, and everyone else—we can all improve our lives somehow. While many have figured out how to excel in a few areas, no one is perfect. The biggest obstacle that prevents people from becoming the best version of themselves is the difficulty in gathering enough mental momentum to escape their current situation. For example, a rocket must fly almost seven miles per second to break free from the Earth's gravitational pull. If it fails to do so, it keeps orbiting until it runs out of fuel and crashes.

Similarly, you can gain the momentum needed to break free from where you are to achieve your best possible future by acknowledging your past and embracing God's acceptance. Moreover, it's crucial to understand that while some of your faults and weaknesses may be real, many may exist *only in your mind!* God's free gifts of mercy and grace help you overcome these *perceived* shortcomings.

Hebrews 4:16
Let us, therefore come boldly unto the throne of grace, that we may obtain mercy, and find grace to help in time of need.

Sometimes, we make it harder to accept God's mercy and grace as we grow because we believe we must meet specific requirements before receiving them. It's similar to thinking that you must clean your car before taking it to the car wash or washing your dishes before putting them in the dishwasher. This belief consumes our thoughts and energy and wastes our time. It dramatically hinders our progress, because we believe we must fix our lives, even before we approach God.

We can never do enough to earn or deserve God's love. We can only receive it freely through Jesus. Even when we try our best to change and face life with faith, there are times when God is not pleased with our actions. However, this does *not* change the fact that He accepts us as we are. As we renew our minds, we begin to see ourselves as receivers of His love and vessels through which He can work. Once we embrace this mindset, we start to accelerate our Becoming!

ACCEPTANCE vs. BECOMING

Being accepted by God and becoming who we're called to be, are two very different things. As stated, God embraces us right where we are, just as we are. God's love, grace, and mercy cover us despite our bad habits, inappropriate actions, and other shortcomings.

2 Timothy 1:9 NIV
He has saved us and called us to a holy life—not because of anything we have done, but because of his own purpose and grace. This grace was given us in Christ Jesus before the beginning of time.

As we identify areas where we need to mature or change, God's acceptance is not a license to sin. However, it gives us the approval and freedom to live accepted while growing!

You might think life isn't changing fast enough for you or is worsening instead of improving. God sometimes allows us to go through challenges, so we'll learn new things or revisit and correct past failures. Whether our challenges are from decisions we've made or required lessons we must embrace to reach our destinies— the key is to *keep believing*. Trust in God no matter how long your transformation takes. As mentioned, God changes us from glory to glory. Growing and improving in life is accelerated when you learn to *embrace* the glory you're already in by controlling and directing your thinking (Philippians 4:8-9 NLT).

**FEEL GOOD ABOUT WHERE YOU ARE!
AS YOU CONTINUE TO LOOK TO JESUS,
YOU'RE TRANSFORMED FROM GLORY TO GLORY!**

The race to your destiny, and eventually to Heaven, will include weights that slow you down, including sin, which tries to stop all forward progress and make you fall.

35

Hebrews 12:1-2 NLT

Therefore, since we are surrounded by such a huge crowd of witnesses to the life of faith, let us strip off every weight that slows us down, especially the sin that so easily trips us up. And let us run with endurance the race God has set before us. [2] We do this by keeping our eyes on Jesus, the champion who initiates and perfects our faith. Because of the joy awaiting Him, He endured the cross, disregarding its shame. Now He is seated in the place of honor beside God's throne.

THE ROAD TO YOUR DESTINY

God recorded every day of our lives *before we were born.* (Psalm 139:16) Our mission is to keep believing THROUGH the times when we don't understand the path. You may think you're disqualified or can't be used by God because of past mistakes or current habits. But God knows your heart and sees who you really are. Destiny is a journey, and your life is made up of seasons. "To everything, there is a season." (Ecclesiastes 3:1). Don't be fooled into thinking that you've failed or that life is over because of your current season!

The Accuser will try to cause you to define yourself through past *failures.* He wants you to think you don't have God's acceptance and favor. Don't be defined by these negative thoughts or what others might say. Be defined by what God says in His Word!

Don't let where you've come from define where you are or where you're *going*. God knows your struggles! He can block the obstacles that prevent you from achieving your purpose. The key is being honest about where you are and sincerely asking God for help. Transparency allows healing and the conscious awareness of your re-established dominion. Once you've acknowledged your limitations and humbly confess to God that you require assistance, He *will* help you!

God has a destiny for you to fulfill and an assignment only you can accomplish. The words you're reading in this book are a part of my assignment. Even though I've not achieved everything I desire or am called to complete, I AM BECOMING! *while being transformed* and making progress.

IT'S OK TO BE "YOU" WHILE YOU BECOME YOU,
BY BECOMING MORE AND MORE LIKE HIM!

Never failing is not required to live a full life, but you can't live a full life if you never try! Get up and live!

I encourage you to accept where you are and embrace your growth and development as you systematically apply the Word to your life by reading and meditating daily. *Keep Becoming!*

Start where you are. Use what you have. Do what you can.
—ARTHUR ASH

–3–

RELATIONSHIP vs. RELIGION

Sir, my concern is not whether God is on our side—
my greatest concern is to be on God's side, for God is always right.
—ABRAHAM LINCOLN

RELATIONSHIP vs. RELIGION

The Merriam-Webster dictionary defines religion as (1) the belief in a god or a group of gods, (2) an organized system of beliefs, ceremonies, and rules used to worship a god or group of gods, (3) an interest, a belief, or an activity which is very important to a person or group.

Religion. In *Merriam-Webster's collegiate dictionary.*
https://www.merriam-webster.com/dictionary/religion

39

Some people say Christianity is a relationship—not a religion. This is partially true. Believers should treat reunion with God as the most important relationship they'll ever have!. You and God, together.

Through this relationship, God empowers us to live our lives as citizens of the Kingdom of God. Notice that I said, "He empowers us," rather than demand that we strive for righteousness, using our abilities. God *desires* a relationship with us. He *wants* us to seek Him.

For example, when I was first introduced to my now-wife, I began pursuing her. It started with an initial conversation, which led to exchanging phone numbers. Frequent, often late-night phone calls led to dates. As we continued to get to know each other, we became closer and closer until we both realized we desired a life together. After many years of marriage, our courtship is still ongoing.

We're to pursue our relationship with God as one does in a marriage. It should be established in love, not obligation. A religious approach to any relationship, marked by excessive rules and ceremonies, can often rob us of experiencing true love!

So how does pursuing a relationship with God allow us to become who we are? The answers came when I felt comfortable enough in my relationship with God to ask Him! He knows everything already, so we won't surprise or catch Him off-guard when we ask questions or mention problems. Religion often causes people to think that God wants them to do something to earn the privilege of access to Him. This is a trick of the Enemy and is not true! God's already provided access and demonstrated His love for us, not based on what we can do for Him, but because of who He is and what He's already done for us in the finished work of Christ.

I had a personal breakthrough when I stopped trying to say and do the right things or please certain people. Instead, I allowed God's Word to help me renew my thinking. I started realizing the joy and privilege of reading words inspired by God, and I began to long for His Presence!

Some people mistake quantity time for quality time in an effort to earn God's acceptance. Have you attempted to work the scripture you read yesterday into your life today? How does it personally apply to you, a family member, or a friend? How can it help you in your current situation? Have you done a word search on it or read different translations to get additional revelation or meaning? Have you prayed for further understanding?

God will open additional revelation to you in the sanctity of your relationship with Him, as you spend time with Him, and discover who He empowers you to be!

Following is an example of how I studied and meditated on a well-known passage of scripture, Matthew 6:30-33.

STUDY NOTES AND ONE OF MY FIRST DECLARATIONS

Matthew 6:30-33 NKJV

Now if God so clothes the grass of the field, which today is, and tomorrow is thrown into the oven, will He not much more clothe you, O you of little faith? [31] "Therefore do not worry, saying, 'What shall we eat?' or 'What shall we drink?' or 'What shall we wear?' [32] For after all these things the Gentiles seek. For your heavenly Father knows that you need all these things. [33] But seek first the Kingdom of God and His righteousness, and all these things shall be added to you.

In the Message Bible, the same passage reads:

Matthew 6:30-33 MSG

If God gives such attention to the appearance of wildflowers—most of which are never even seen—don't you think he'll attend to you, take pride in you, do his best for you? What I'm trying to do here is to get you to relax, to not be so preoccupied with getting, so you can respond to God's giving. People who don't know God and the way he works, fuss over these things, but you know both God and how he works. Steep your life in God-reality, God-initiative, God-provisions. Don't worry about missing out. You'll find all your everyday human concerns will be met.

I'm sure many of you have read this passage hundreds of times. I've heard countless sermons preached on "Seeking first the Kingdom of God." I've listened to several recommendations about how to apply it to my life. "Pray for an hour—this is what Jesus did." "Read this many chapters and that many books of the Bible a day because the entrance of His Word gives light!" "Devote the first 2.4 hours of your day to God—it's only 10%." "Read your Bible first thing in the morning," and many other recommendations. While these might be useful suggestions, let's explore an additional perspective.

"These things," mentioned in verse 33, represent life's basic necessities: food and clothing. Too often, Jesus' words have been taken out of context and used to suggest that all material things will come to us—if we, His children, would seek Him first. However, this is not the full meaning of the passage.

Does God provide other things besides food and clothes to His children? Of course He does! The following scriptures represent two examples of many which support this fact.

Matthew 7:11 NLT
So, if you sinful people know how to give good gifts to your children, how much more will your heavenly Father give good gifts, to those who ask him.

Psalm 37:4-5 NLT

Take delight in the LORD, and he will give you your heart's desires. [5] Commit everything you do to the LORD. Trust him, and he will help you.

In Chapters 5, 6, and 7 in the book of Matthew, the central message is to instruct believers on *how* to enter the Kingdom of Heaven. It addresses worldly concerns like food, drink, and material possessions, and assures us that God will fill all His children's needs. We're encouraged to shift our attitude about temporary things and prioritize the Kingdom instead.

SEEKING BY PRAYER

It's wonderful to get up and pray to our Father daily. It's one of the best ways to start a day. In the Acknowledgments at the front of the book, I mentioned the 6 a.m. (5 a.m. for me) morning online prayer and how it played a major role in helping me develop my spiritual foundation.

I can't tell you how long I pray every day. In fact, I'm a walking prayer meeting most days! I pray all day! I pray in the morning, when I wake up, with no set-time length, but this changes as desired or required. I pray throughout the day about decisions I must make or things I must do. I pray to thank God for any good or great things happening in my life, family, and business. When I face situations that need improvement, I pray to thank God for favor and for all things to work out for good. I regularly pray and

44

repent for any known or unknown sins I've committed. Lastly, sometimes I pray just to say, "Thank You, Father!"

As with any relationship, a conversation is not a monologue—it's a dialogue. Praying to God is no different. I often pause to think and listen. If I don't get an immediate response, I hope and expect to receive answers during my day.

In addition to hearing an inner voice for direction and confirmation, the answers often come from people or through other normal daily life circumstances and encounters. I might see a headline on a billboard that speaks directly to me. I've heard lyrics of songs that seem to confirm a decision. I've received calls or text messages from friends and acquaintances, who share something from a great book they're reading, or about a scene in a movie they've recently watched. I've even received confirmation from emails and social media.

> *People see God every day, they just don't recognize him.*
> —PEARL BAILEY

SEEKING, BY READING THE WORD

Whether you read your Bible first thing in the morning or at a set time of day, the intake of the Word helps us live life better and to its fullest.

Matthew 4:4 NLT

But Jesus told him, 'No! The Scriptures say, People do not live by bread alone, but by every word, that comes from the mouth of God.'

Joshua 1:1 MSG

And don't for a minute let this Book of The Revelation be out of mind. Ponder and meditate on it day and night, making sure you practice everything written in it. Then you'll get where you're going; then you'll succeed.

Why are so many people challenged when it comes to reading the Bible? Why do they often fall asleep or struggle to discover how they can apply what they've read to their lives?

It's good to set a daily time to read God's Word, but are you allowing it to change your thinking? Do you ever feel compelled to stop what you're doing and read a scripture or declare how it's shaping your future? Have you ever turned off the TV to get into His Word just "because?" It's a great plan to start from the beginning of the Bible, challenging yourself to achieve daily, weekly, or monthly reading goals. What works best for you to ensure daily intake of His Word?

Seeking God First begins with developing a focus and lifestyle of building an intimate, loving relationship with Him. Let me reiterate—nothing we receive in our relationship with God is because of anything we've done or can do. It's only because of our relationship with God that *anything* is possible.

Below is an example of a Declaration I created, which included some of the revelations I received while studying and meditating on Matthew 6:33, and several other supporting scriptures.

DRAWING NEAR

I start my day by once again making You the center of my focus.

Father, I say, I'm not always given the opportunity to pick or choose the type or timing of the challenges I encounter, but today I start my day by once again making You the center of my focus. I seek You, and give You my attention first! I won't allow any known or newly encountered "giants" to distract me from acknowledging and DRAWING NEAR to You and Your amazing love for me! Who gives me the boldness to come to You with a clear conscience, whether I created the problem or it chose me? Jesus Christ! I accept and acknowledge that He alone allows me to enter into Your mercy and grace whenever I need You. Thank You, Father! I AM BECOMING! In Jesus' name!

1 Samuel 17:4-11, Matthew 6:33, James 4:7-10 MSG, Hebrews 4:14-16, John 1:1

The study and supporting declaration above illustrate one of the ways I read and learn from the Word of God. Part #2 of this book is a collection of declarations born from hours of prayer, immersive reading, spirited discussions with friends, and studying God's Word. I encourage you to establish a daily routine that suits your needs. Even if you discover or create just one new technique or method that aids you in incorporating the Word of God into your everyday situations, it can radically impact your life and strengthen your relationship with Him.

I firmly believe that God desires us to make the most of each day and every moment, regardless of changes in life circumstances.

Watering your life with God's Word can mean the difference between being buried by circumstances or being productively planted into this life—growing to bring forth the harvest of your purpose! God wants us to *keep Becoming!*

I'm unfinished. I'm unfixed. And the reality is, that's where
God meets me, in the mess of my life, in the unfixedness, in the
brokenness. I thought He did the opposite, He got rid of all that stuff.
But if you read the Bible, if you look at it at all, He constantly was
showing up in people's lives, at the worst possible time of their life.
—MIKE YACONELLI

−4−

HOW TO BELIEVE
DESPITE THE FIVE-D'S

Success is not final, failure is not fatal —
it's the courage to continue that counts.
—WINSTON CHURCHILL

God placed within each of us the potential and authority to accomplish our assigned purpose and vision. He also gave us the desire, passion, and wisdom to continually make adjustments as we navigate life during the progress of BECOMING.

Suppose you have poorly defined goals or none at all, feel hindered or blocked in your progress, or are very excited because you're excelling or already reaching your daily objectives. Regardless of where you are, you were given the power of God's Word to *create, maintain, and change your world!*

So, what's holding you back? How do you get unstuck and stay on course? You may wake up with good intentions and plans, but things continually break your focus or tempt you to change directions. How do you keep moving forward, even after you've experienced setback after setback? The answer is—Life and Death are in the power of the tongue. (Proverbs 18:21) Right thinking leads to right believing and right speaking. This always produces right results.

RIGHT THINKING LEADS TO RIGHT BELIEVING AND SPEAKING. THIS PRODUCES RIGHT RESULTS

How do you consistently grow and progress to become who you're called to be?

THE RIGHT PERSPECTIVE

BECOMING you first involves unscrambling your life into several foundational areas. I call it "silencing the noise of life." The first step is to categorize your daily life activities into one or more of the following areas:

- **Spiritual** (Foundational beliefs and values—the real you)
- **Physical** (Health, fitness, proper nutrition)
- **Family** (Relatives, close inner-circle friends)
- **Financial** (Business, savings, budgeting, investments)
- **Educational** (Learning, personal development, teaching)
- **Vocational** (Career, occupation, talent, calling)
- **Social** (Friends, community, other relationships)

I found it easier to unravel and navigate issues as I viewed them from this perspective. This strategy allowed me to identify strengths, weaknesses, and patterns. It didn't always result in solutions—I had a lot of "baggage to unpack!"

As I addressed my issues "from the outside-in," I eventually realized I was overlooking beliefs, feelings, and emotions, which were key factors to personal growth and development. I didn't always understand the root causes of my problems or find practical solutions to them. This "outside-in" strategy did work, but it wasn't complete. I still experienced struggle, wasted efforts, and inconsistent success.

LIVING FROM THE "OUTSIDE-IN"

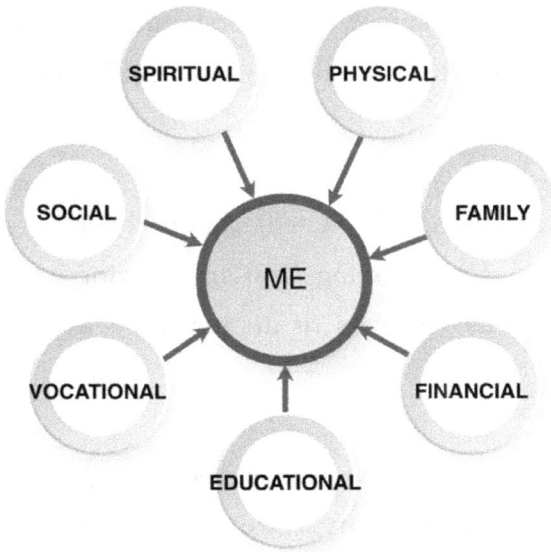

STRUGGLE, WASTED EFFORT, INCONSISTENT SUCCESS
Diagram #1

While in college, after I became a believer, like many of you, I was given a list of guidelines that supposedly defined the "Christian way of life" Over time, I discovered I was prone to self-criticism and judgment toward others who didn't adhere to every item on the list. Nowadays, it's more common to take a relaxed approach toward guidelines and principles, as many faith-based institutions try to appeal to new generations and demographics. This newfound acceptance may lead some to misunderstand or not fully comprehend that having a relationship with God still involves embracing a new life founded on Godly principles. The key is to renew our minds and live according to His Word, established in love.

I found that outward obedience, or the act of complying with rules without internal agreement or understanding, often lead to me trying to earn God's favor. It did not necessarily address concerns of the heart.

God's love, as previously stated, cannot be earned! It's not dependent on the good feelings that arise during worship—when we experience His kindness or an increased awareness of His presence.

While questions about my desires, feelings, past failures, and successes began to have clarity, I struggled to maintain balance. I felt life was a never-ending game of whack-a-mole. As soon as I identified a problem in one area, another would pop up somewhere else while I tried to figure out a solution to the first issue.

Some people have incredible success in certain areas of their lives. While this is admirable, excelling in one aspect does not necessarily prevent them from neglecting or struggling in others. In fact, great success may overshadow or conceal major challenges or character flaws. It frequently defies understanding when the news covers shocking and disturbing stories about the troubles of the business and political elite, superstar athletes, and award-winning entertainers. Their struggles reveal how little we really know about their mindsets and confirm that NO ONE is immune to the trials and challenges of life. We all have issues that can only be shaped and improved by applying biblical principles.

THEN vs. NOW

Our Spiritual life should be our number one priority. If it isn't, we may struggle to achieve balance but never achieve it at all. This battle is because the state of our spiritual life qualifies or prevents us from walking in dominion. (Genesis 1:28 & Psalm 8:6)

Regardless of your socio-economic status, your physical life impacts your family life, which affects your financial life, influences your educational life, thwarts your social life, etc.

Our renewed spiritual life is not just an area we manage, as illustrated in Diagram #1. Our spiritual life *is our true life*! It directs every other area and empowers us to live—from the inside-out. (See Diagram #2)

Living a spirit-led life does not mean immediately living a problem-free or perfect life. However, it's the best way to maintain lasting, overall balance.

THE SPIRIT-LED LIFE ENCOMPASSES EVERYTHING.
LIVING FROM THE "INSIDE-OUT"

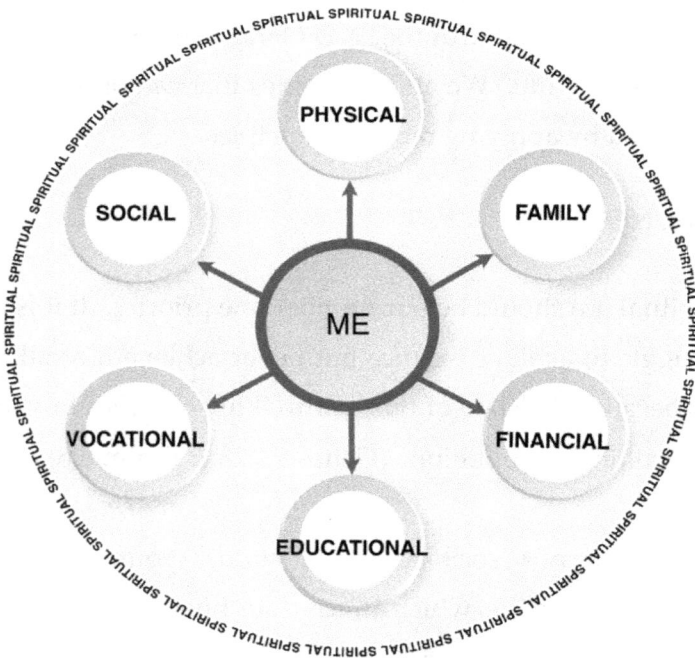

THIS IS OUR TRUE IDENTITY
Diagram #2

Matthew 6:33-34 MSG

[33] "Steep your life in God-reality, God-initiative, God-provisions. Don't worry about missing out. You'll find all your everyday human concerns will be met. [34] "Give your entire attention to what God is doing right now, and don't get worked up about what may or may not happen tomorrow. God will help you deal with whatever hard things come up when the time comes.

So, how do believers break-free from the invisible chains which hold them down in each area? How do we elevate ourselves above circumstances which constantly threaten to keep us from reaching our full potential? What "flips the switch" and frees us to make steady, measurable progress?

I've discovered that it's not always big shifts that hold us back or propel us forward. It's a series of *consistently-targeted adjustments* which build or weaken the foundation of who we are.

I've also realized that being a believer does not mean the absence of challenges or the lack of struggles. Instead, it's an opportunity to acknowledge God's presence as we deal with everything that comes our way.

IN THE MIDDLE

Starting and finishing goals is exciting and fulfilling, but the journey is often ignored or not discussed. In a few pages, you'll find a collection of IN THE MIDDLE studies summarized into Declarations (Prayers). I've given them the name "I AM BECOMING!" to constantly be reminded that as I immerse myself in reading, studying, meditating on, and embracing God's Word, I'm continually transforming myself into a new person who resembles Him, more and more—which is who I was created to be!

Each declaration reflects a bible study I embarked upon to target circumstances, opportunities, feelings, and thoughts that required mind renewal. I designed them to give quick, issue-specific glances at God's perspectives. These studies ranged from a few hours to a few months. I didn't limit the length of study or review time. They were all framed to help me shape my thinking, words, and actions. Walking in dominion authority remains my objective.

The short declarations are written in the first person, to be spoken aloud, and used to silence the relentless daily onslaught of negative thoughts and influences. This is just one method of embracing Paul's pleading in Romans 12:1-2.

Romans 12:1-2 MSG
So here's what I want you to do, God helping you: Take your everyday, ordinary life—your sleeping, eating, going-to-work, and walking-around life—and place it before God as an offering. Embracing what God does for you is the best thing you can do for him. Don't become so well-adjusted to your culture that you fit into it without even thinking. Instead, fix your

attention on God.   You'll be changed from the inside out.   Readily
recognize what he wants from you, and quickly respond to it.   Unlike the
culture around you, always dragging you down to its level of immaturity,
God brings the best out of you, [and] develops well-formed maturity in
you.

THE FIGHT

Although this is not an all-inclusive list, the Enemy cleverly uses these five strategies (The Five-D's) to carry out his Obstruction Mission:

1. Destroy
2. Distract
3. Discourage
4. Derail
5. Discredit

I'm not suggesting these five categories represent his only strategies.   They merely represent methods I've observed being used against me and others most often.

The fact that you're reading this book means that you haven't been physically destroyed — yet. If you've never accepted Jesus Christ as your personal savior, I invite you to visit the Appendix at the back of this book to take that step today.

The Bible tells us in Hebrews 2:14 and 1 John 3:8 that Jesus *finished* it! That means the Accuser has already been defeated!

Our battle is to continually remind ourselves and the powers of darkness that Jesus has already won! As believers, it's vital to know that you don't fight *for* victory—you fight from a position *of* victory!

AS A BELIEVER, YOU DON'T FIGHT *FOR* VICTORY— YOU FIGHT FROM A POSITION *OF* VICTORY!

THE FIVE-D's DEFINED

DESTROY - de· stroy | 1: to ruin the structure, organic existence, or condition of   2a: to put out of existence: KILL   b: NEUTRALIZE c: ANNIHILATE, VANQUISH*

The Enemy would like to prevent you from reaching your destiny, keep you from accepting Jesus Christ as your savior—or outright kill you before completing any of the above—if he could.

DISTRACT - dis· tract | 1a: to draw or direct (something, such as someone's attention) to a different object or in different directions at the same time   b: to turn aside: DIVERT   2: to stir up or confuse with conflicting emotions or motives*

Let's consider out-of-the-blue phone calls, a rash of unexpected problems, and negative people emerging from your past.

If focus is one of the keys to success, then broken focus is one of the leading causes of failure. If someone can't beat you facing you head-on, beware when they run beside you, quietly whispering in your ear. That's the strategy of distraction—to divert.

> *The best way to steal a man's dream is to give him another dream.*
> —UNKNOWN

DISCOURAGE - dis· cour· age | 1: to deprive of courage or confidence: DISHEARTEN. 2a: to hinder by disfavoring. b: to dissuade or attempt to dissuade from doing something.*

Inconsistent movement and forward progress—*Start, Stop, Start, Delay*— is similar to what happens when traveling by car. You experience wind resistance, potholes, mechanical problems, and other challenges as a byproduct of moving! In life, the Enemy attempts to amplify the obstacles so that *they become your focus*— instead of your desired destination. The issues you face become prominent and begin to speak to you. Nothing should speak louder to us than the Word of God! Discouragement can also cause us to create scenarios that exist only in our minds, slowing our progress.

DERAIL - de· rail | 1: to cause to run off the rails, 2a: to obstruct the progress of: FRUSTRATE b: to upset the stability or composure of.*

Derailment is a byproduct of discouragement. When you're discouraged, you make slight or inconsistent progress, but you still have the potential for advancement. A derailment eliminates the possibility of forward progress. A train derailment, for example, completely prevents the cargo from being delivered. Even if it remains upright and intact, the engine becomes useless potential and power without potency because it's off-the-track.

DISCREDIT - dis· cred· it | 1: to refuse to accept as true or accurate: DISBELIEVE   2: to cause disbelief in the accuracy or authority of 3: to deprive of good repute: DISGRACE Discrediting you.*

After we achieve a measurable degree of success, things happen which may take away our voice and influence. We "win the race," but no one cheers or wants our advice. Discrediting occurs when someone does or is accused of doing something illegal, shameful, or disgraceful. It can result from a pattern of behavior, a series of events, or lies. Regardless of how you are discredited, you become a voice without volume.

THE ANSWER

The good news is that God's Word can help us get and stay free from all of the Five-D Strategies.

We're told to think about "good things" in Philippians 4:8-9 because so many "bad things" vie for attention and try to harness our creative resources.

Philippians 4:8-9 NLT

"And now, dear brothers and sisters, one final thing. Fix your thoughts on what is true, and honorable, and right, and pure, and lovely, and admirable. Think about things that are excellent and worthy of praise. [9] Keep putting into practice all you learned and received from me—everything you heard from me and saw me doing. Then the God of peace will be with you."

THE CLIMB

To prepare for a climb like the one illustrated on the cover, mountaineers must first know what kind of mountain they'll be climbing to develop a plan, including a hydration strategy. People have different stamina and energy levels. The amount of water they bring depends on several factors, such as the difficulty and duration of the climb, the climate, and their personal needs. The best thing they can do to complete the climb is listen to their bodies.

Believers, like mountaineers, must plan when and how much of the water of God's Word (Ephesians 5:26 ESV) is required, based upon need-driven conditions and circumstances.

Philippians 2:12 encourages believers to work out their personal salvation with "fear and trembling." Working it out does NOT mean, working to earn salvation. It means that the free gift we receive from God, is released by faith. *Faith* does the work, not us!

Faith comes by hearing the Word of God (Romans 10:17). When we consistently study of the Bible, we encounter God's life-changing presence and gain numerous other benefits.

Today's world is full of videos, books, motivational speakers, and even preachers sharing tips-and-tricks, which promise to lead us to secrets or shortcuts to this or that. From time-management to relationships, fitness to finances, and almost any other subject, someone boasts he has *the* quickest and shortest path to success.

We can get a meal or order a car at the click of a button. Almost anything can be delivered to our door in two days or less. We can instantly share our innermost thoughts and feelings online and get feedback from people worldwide in seconds. We have become conditioned to exert little effort to get desired results quickly. Unfortunately, this way of thinking has set similar expectations for believers concerning the impact and change one receives from reading the Bible.

Can God respond instantly to our needs, wants, and desires? Absolutely! Do some things take time and involve other people? Yes. Does God cause Divine Delays? Sometimes. Maybe He's giving us time to confess, repent, and change our thinking— to *Believe* and *Act!*

Life's journey is filled with growth opportunities. And what we don't learn from God by explicit instruction, He can reveal through the lessons woven into our experiences. Whether these encounters are joyful or challenging, God wants us to declare and pray during delays. The bottom line is *we should not lose heart.* The faith walk involves believing not seeing. (2 Corinthians 5:7)

WHAT WE DON'T LEARN FROM GOD BY INSTRUCTION WILL OFTEN BE TAUGHT THROUGH EXPERIENCES

READING & SPEAKING THE DECLARATIONS

This book is designed to be one of the most valuable and practical tools for helping believers use God's Word to change their thinking. It's intended to provide an additional way for you to view your world, inspire increased hunger for the Word of God, and offer a new method and tool to feed that hunger. THIS BOOK IS NOT A SUBSTITUTE FOR BIBLE READING—IT'S A TOOL TO INSPIRE IT!

The I AM BECOMING! Program is just one method I've used to help me build my Kingdom-of-God Dominion mindset. The most essential elements of the declarations are the supporting scriptures and your renewed mind, which results from reading and applying them to your life. The key is the *re-newing* of your mind!

The opening pages and Part #1 have given you a proven starting point to grasp the foundation and context of this book. Part #2, the declarations, can be read in any order needed. It's like the Star Wars media franchise—the declarations complement each other, and the order doesn't matter. The Appendix contains a topical and alphabetized index for easy reference. The beauty lies in the flexibility to explore, discover, and revisit topics as desired.

Try reading one or more of the supporting scriptures, speaking the declarations, and then re-reading and speaking them again as often as you need throughout the day. Work the Word into your life— especially for specific challenges or opportunities! To determine your focus, follow your heart and God's prompting. As stated, I focused on some topics for months when creating the declarations!

My strategy for developing the I AM BECOMING! Program was to discover how God thinks about my daily life, the things I desire, and the areas in which I need to grow. I designed it to systematically plant the seed of the Word of God into my mind so

I could change my thinking. As this happened, I began to use other talents, gifts, creativity, and imagination to focus on becoming a *willing participant* in the creation of the world God has promised me.

> Speak to your future daily with targeted declarations. Don't just give attention to the struggle; call things that are *NOT* as if they *ARE*! (Romans 4:17) Great creations don't just happen. They're *designed*.

Understanding your assignment, running your race, and being comfortable with whom God made you to be will allow you to create your world, touch other people, and bring true fulfillment to your life.

As you study God's Word to renew your mind, I encourage you to create additional declarations and apply them as needed to your situations.

How can we know we're on the right path in a world where many opinions and ideas influence our destiny? We know because it's measured by the things we store in our hearts, in our thoughts, and released by our actions. Its evidence is found by embracing the love and Word of God and the way we love ourselves and others. If we live in the knowledge that we're created in the image of God, then we can honestly say, *I AM BECOMING!*

> PRAYER
>
> Thank You, Father, for wisdom, favor, and discernment. Thank you especially for showing me how to maximize my time, talents, and other resources. This allows me to demonstrate Your stability in an unstable world. Continue to change and develop me so I keep progressing toward my purpose. I AM BECOMING! more and more like You every day! In Jesus' name!

Every soldier must know, before he goes into battle, how the little battle he is to fight, fits into the larger picture, and how the success of his fighting, will influence the battle as a whole.
—BENARD LAW MONTGOMERY

To receive a complimentary template for easily creating effective personal declarations, please visit dwayneAwalker.com/template

*Destroy, Distract, Discourage, Derail, and Discredit. (n.d.) In Merriam-Webster's collegiate dictionary. http://www.merriam-webster.com/dictionary/Destroy, Distract, Discourage, Derail, and Discredit

PART 2

DESTROY

IN THE BEGINNING

I speak life, structure, and multiplication into my world today!

Father, I say, just as you spoke to a formless, empty entity and made it the canvas for a world of creations, I speak to my day, life, and world today. You looked past what was and spoke into existence your desires. You saw past the darkness and spoke light into being, followed by the consistent and deliberate use of your words, to ignite other latent potential. Your words created every living thing, including me, your masterpiece. I will replicate your pattern for creation IN THE BEGINNING of my day today and whenever I experience any void, unshaped, or dark areas in my life. You created a fresh, lush, fertile world that would not only sustain but multiply. I too, speak life, structure, and multiplication into my world today! I AM BECOMING! In Jesus' name!

Genesis 1:1-3, Genesis 1:11-12, Genesis 1:24-25, Genesis 1:26-28,
Psalm 139:13-18, John 1:1-5, John 1:14, Matthew 12:37, Proverbs 18:21

_____

_____

_____

_____

_____

ANCHORS

*Pull up any invisible anchors of unforgiveness
that impede and prevent forward progress.*

Father, I say, as I begin my day today, I will continue to systematically identify and pull up any invisible ANCHORS of unforgiveness that impede and prevent my forward progress. I realize that my forgiveness of others is achieved by faith, not by how they respond to me or my feelings. You are the source of my comfort and peace, not my actions or feelings! I am determined to be an agent of change and influence in my environment rather than passively allowing it to shape me I am dominating my day with your Word and love! I am growing, moving forward, and I AM BECOMING! In Jesus' name!

Mark 11:25, Matthew 18:21-22, 2 Corinthians 5:7, Romans 15:1

_____

_____

_____

_____

_____

_____

PERSPECTIVE MATTERS

Perspective matters, but only the one that I have of you and your love!

Father, I say, today I will embrace the same perspective that David took when he faced Goliath—I refuse to look at the size of any problem, but rather I will focus on the capabilities and size of you, my God! When it comes to my dreams, I will firmly resist the temptation to diminish them in order to align with an immature, underdeveloped, or diminished self-image. Instead, I will persistently explore, accept, and wholeheartedly celebrate my true identity in you. The size of any problem pales in comparison to the size of your solutions. I will expand the size of my dreams to fit the ever-expanding size of my "God-esteem." Yes, PERSPECTIVE MATTERS, but only the one that I have of you and your love, mercy, grace, size, and capabilities! I AM BECOMING! In Jesus' name!

1 Samuel 17:25-26, 1 Samuel 17:34-37, 1 Samuel 17:45-47

_____

_____

_____

_____

_____

AWAKE

I'm spiritually awake and continually hear your voice.

Father, I say, thank you for making my spirit alive in you. As you bless my hours to turn them into days, weeks, months, and years, I also thank you for helping me to stay spiritually AWAKE. Help me never to grow dull to your presence, to continually hear your voice, and to always be aware of what You are doing in my day-to-day life. I'm relying on Your Word and Spirit to lead me to the people, places, and things that are truly important today. My ability to openly acknowledge others is only possible because I continually invite and accept Your love into my heart. I am AWAKE, and I AM BECOMING! In Jesus' name!

Ephesians 2:1-10 (NIV), Mark 13:33-37, Matthew 26:38-46 NLT, Ephesians 5:1-2, 14-19, Isaiah 40:31

_____

_____

_____

_____

_____

MORE THAN A CONQUEROR

Help me to see myself and others through your eyes.

Father, I say, today I will look past any problems that I've been through, that I'm going through, or that I might encounter in the future. I not only believe that you are my healer, provider, and counselor, but I know that you have made me MORE THAN A CONQUEROR!! I refuse to be discouraged or walk in fear, because I know you are forever with me! Winning is given, and my focus is now on running up the score! Nothing is too difficult for you! Help me to constantly see myself and others through your eyes today. I AM BECOMING! In Jesus' name!

Exodus 15:26, Philippians 4:19, Psalm 16:7-8 (MSG), Romans 8:37, Jeremiah 32:27, Isaiah 41:10

_____

_____

_____

_____

_____

_____

LAUNCHING OUT

*I won't allow fear, distraction, habit, or religion
to prevent me from making progress towards my destiny today.*

Father, I say, by following the leading of the Holy Spirit, I will launch out today and do something that will advance me towards my destiny. Whether it's a business-related task, reaching out to repair or establish relationships, or introducing someone to Christ, I will faithfully embrace advancement. I'll keep my eyes on Jesus as I step out of my comfort zone. I won't allow fear, distraction, habit, or religion to prevent me from making deliberate and measurable progress towards my destiny, today. I AM BECOMING! In Jesus' name!

Luke 5:1-11, 2 Corinthians 5:7, Matthew 14:22-33

_____

_____

_____

_____

_____

_____

IN YOU

In You, I'm empowered to capture, shape, and control my thoughts!

Father, I say, IN YOU I'm free, I'm forgiven, I'm a joint heir, I'm Your child, and made clean and righteous. I'm brand new, wonderfully made, a unique masterpiece, and I'm never alone. I'm a temple for the Holy Spirit, and I'm able to live, move, and possess Your promises! You've empowered me to be able to capture, shape, and control my thoughts! Thank you that I can walk free from fear, and for equipping me to do everything I need to do to win! IN YOU, I'm more than a conqueror! I AM BECOMING! In Jesus' name!

IN YOU I AM:

Free - *Galatians 5:1*
A Joint Heir - *Romans 8:17*
Healed - *1 Peter 2:24*
Brand New - *2 Corinthians 5:17*
Never alone - *Deuteronomy 31:8*
Able to live - *Acts 17:28*
Protected - Psalm 23:4
Made Clean - *Isaiah 1:18*
Your Child - *John 1:12*
Righteous - *2 Corinthians 5:21*
Masterpiece - *Ephesian 2:10*
A temple - *1 Corinthians 6:19*
Able to shape my thoughts - *2 Corinthians 10:5*
Can do all things - *Philippians 4:13*
More than a conqueror - *Numbers 13:30, Romans 8:37*

DEADLY INTENTIONS

God's promise of victory came with instructions.

Father, I say, when I accepted Jesus, I was given access to your armor and told that I was in a war. Your directive to put that armor on, let me know that there would be a conflict. Thank you for your instructions and the promise of victory! The Enemy is already defeated, but he is desperate. The war he wages on my flesh and mind intensifies when I advance in the spirit. So I woke up this morning armed and with DEADLY INTENTIONS! I'm excited and thankful that I will have a good day, but I realize that the Enemy never takes vacations, so neither will I. I am advancing, and I AM BECOMING! In Jesus' name!

2 Corinthians 10:3-6, 1 Corinthians 15:57, Revelation 12:7-11, Colossians 2:15, Ephesians 6:10-17, James 4:4-8

_____

_____

_____

_____

_____

_____

I AM WELL ABLE!

*My focus is on the size, capabilities, and
the omnipresence of you, my God.*

Father, I say forgive me for being distracted by cares instead of reminding myself of the benefits of my covenant with you. Forgive me for allowing myself to be intimidated by the size and presence of "giants" instead of fixing my gaze upon Your immense power, capabilities, and ever-present nature, my God! Your promise did not come with a "giant free" guarantee, but it did come with an already-won victory! Faith always delivers a good report; while an evil report is the offspring of doubt. By faith, I proclaim that I AM WELL ABLE to possess the land and advance closer to my destiny today! I AM BECOMING! In Jesus' name!

Deuteronomy 11:8-9, 1 John 2:15-17, Colossians 3:2, Luke 8:14-15, Hebrews 8:6-12, Galatians 3:6-29

_____

_____

_____

_____

_____

HELLO GIANTS!

I have been uniquely qualified to finish and succeed!

Father, I say today, as I progress towards my destiny, any "giants" I may encounter will be viewed as confirmation of my advancement. HELLO GIANTS! I won't be intimidated by your size, nor discouraged by your presence. I realize that you want to discourage, distract, or destroy me, to keep me from finishing, but I will remain focused on my objectives! Father, as I embrace your promises and defeat giants, I refuse to be negatively influenced by unqualified people or false opportunities. For not only did you call me, but you have also uniquely qualified me to finish and succeed! I am achieving and advancing, and I AM BECOMING! In Jesus' name!

Number 13:25-33, Isaiah 41:10, Job 17:9

_____

_____

_____

_____

_____

YOU FORGOT

Peace and freedom don't give me a license to sin,
but rather, they give me permission to live free, in You!

Father, I say, when Jesus said, "It is finished," on the cross, He forever paid the price for all my sins—those of the past, present, and future! I believe and embrace the fact that after I accepted Him as my personal Savior, YOU FORGOT! I was not required to "get right," before "You made me right." I came to you just as I was, regardless of my strengths, weaknesses, problems, addictions, good or bad habits, flaws, etc. I'm made new, and free in you, and as I renew my mind and get to know You and Your Word, I'm made free from anything that has held me back or down. Your mercy and grace are incomprehensible. This peace and freedom are not a license to sin, but rather it is permission, for me to live free in You, while I grow and change! I AM BECOMING! In Jesus' name!

Hebrews 8:12, John 19:28–30, John 8:32, 2 John 1:3, 2 Corinthians 5:17, Romans 12:1-2

ALL DAY CELEBRATION

*Anything that I can see is temporary,
but my life in you will last forever.*

Father, I say nothing will keep me from experiencing, expressing, and having an ALL-DAY CELEBRATION about my relationship with you today. I will know when and how to use the creative ability you gave me at birth, to speak and create. I won't allow this ability to be idle, hampered, or hijacked by anything I face today. Anything I can see is temporary, but my life in you will last forever. I AM BECOMING! In Jesus' name!

Ephesians 3:20, 2 Corinthians 4:18, Philippians 4:4 NKJV

_____

_____

_____

_____

_____

_____

_____

EVERYTHING

I don't fight for victory; I fight from a position of victory!

Father, I say, thank you, that I don't have to refight the battle for salvation, healing, peace, or prosperity. I couldn't win them anyway. My focus and belief are in Your Son Jesus Christ and His finished work. The foundation of EVERYTHING I need or want from You is birthed out of this relationship. I acknowledge that the faith to get healed, to prosper, to mend relationships, etc., is the same faith that I used to get saved. No, I don't fight for victory; I fight from a position of victory! Jesus already finished it! I AM BECOMING! In Jesus' name!

John 17:4, Matthew 8:17, Mark 5:36, Ephesians 6:10-16

_____

_____

_____

_____

_____

_____

_____

OVERTAKE & OVERTAKEN

I will pursue and without fail, overtake, and recover anything that has been lost or stolen from me.

Father, I say, I will remain focused on Jesus as I run my "destiny race," with stamina, strength, and persistence. With your guidance, I will let go of or adjust my relationships and attitudes toward people, places, or things that slow me down. I will be OVERTAKEN by your blessings as I listen to, hear, and do what you say. On your cue, I will pursue and, "without fail," OVERTAKE and recover anything that has been lost or stolen from me. My enemies are OVERTAKEN with "endless ruin" while your blessings OVERTAKE me. To be overtaken, while I overtake — only you could make this happen, Father! I embrace, appreciate, and celebrate your presence! I AM BECOMING! In Jesus' name!

Hebrews 12:1-4, 1 Samuel 30:8-20, Isaiah 43:14-21, Psalm 9:6, Deuteronomy 28:2-14

_____

_____

_____

_____

FAITHFUL BELIEF

At my birth, your blessings started forever chasing me!

Father, I say, before I was born, you not only knew everything about me, but you also made provisions for all the plans of my life —my destiny. At my birth, your blessings started forever chasing me! Unlike the old covenant, which required me to "do," then "qualify" for your blessings, Jesus Christ, Your Son fulfilled every requirement of the law. Now, by FAITHFUL BELIEF and acceptance, I too receive the benefits of having obeyed every aspect of your law. Not only am I pursued by your provision, but I am also overtaken by everything necessary for me to prosper! My health, family, relationships, and finances are whole! I AM BECOMING! In Jesus' name!

Jeremiah 1:5, Matthew 5:17-18, Deuteronomy 28:1-2, Genesis 26:12-25, Hebrews 8:7-12, 3 John 1:2

_____

_____

_____

_____

_____

SMALL VICTORIES

Small victories are the bricks that pave the road to greater success,
and are leading me to my destiny.

Father, I say, thank you for the SMALL VICTORIES in my life that don't always get acknowledged or celebrated. I express my gratitude for these victories, no matter how seemingly insignificant they may be, as they serve as both the catalyst and the outcome of my growing faith. They also represent the seeds for future bountiful harvests. Large and fast victories are great, but I want you to know that I also appreciate *all* advancement. I realize that SMALL VICTORIES are the bricks that pave the road to greater success, and are leading me to my destiny. Thank you! I AM BECOMING! In Jesus' name!

Romans 12:3 (MSG), Romans 4:17 (MSG), Luke 19:20-23,
2 Corinthians 9:6

_____

_____

_____

_____

_____

SPLASH

My goal is to demonstrate your presence and power
in every area of my life.

Father, I say, today I will lean on and trust only in you, as I engage my day. My first and primary focus is to acknowledge your presence and welcome your involvement. My goal is not wealth or fame, but rather to demonstrate your presence and power in my everyday life. Let any success or influence that I experience be recognized as the result of my relationship with you. You empower me to make a SPLASH as I create, shape, and influence my day, with your Word. I AM BECOMING! In Jesus' name!

Matthew 6:33, 1 Corinthians 1:26-31, Luke 16:9-12,
1 Corinthians 2:3-4

_____

_____

_____

_____

_____

_____

STORMS

I use your Word to stand strong, change the atmosphere,
and create calm during every storm.

Father, I say, if I experience STORMS in any area of my life today, I won't remain passive or silent and just "ride them out." I will use the authority and instructions you have bestowed upon me through your Word to stand firm, change the atmosphere, and bring about calm! My environment won't determine my aspirations or attitudes. I will walk by faith and not by sight, as I form and shape my day with faith-filled words, just as you did when you created this world and the universe. STORMS often reveal weaknesses, but they also confirm strengths. In the face of any STORM, I will rest in your strength, Father! I AM BECOMING! In Jesus' name!

Ephesians 6:10, Mark 4:35-41, 2 Corinthians 5:7, Genesis 1:1-31

_____

_____

_____

_____

_____

WALKING OUT

I purpose to use any headwinds of resistance that I face
to strengthen my resilience and reliance on you.

Father, I say today, as I engage others, I will remind myself that it's not about me. Although my needs and desires are real and important to me, I'm learning that your heart and love are truly all about giving. Discovering and uncovering my talents and gifts allow me to sow, share, and help the expansion of your Kingdom. As I'm WALKING OUT my life, I purpose to use any headwinds of resistance that I face, to strengthen my resilience and reliance on you. I acknowledge that I can't do anything on my own and that when I'm weak, I'm strong in you. I AM BECOMING! In Jesus' name!

Luke 14:15-35, Matthew 25:14-30, John 15:4-7, 2 Corinthians 12:10

_____

_____

_____

_____

_____

_____

DISTRACT

UNSTUCK

Faithful actions have a greater reward than good intentions.

Father, I say thank you for enabling me to get UNSTUCK! As I speak to my world today, I realize that faithful actions have a greater reward than good intentions. As I reflect, analyze, contemplate, and make adjustments, I am grateful to realize that all change and momentum begin with me, resting in you. I'm not trusting in past victories, nor hindered by prior defeats. I'm looking at the new things you are doing. Your presence and glory are my focus, not my circumstances! I now see challenges differently as I believe and speak. I will repeat this action over and over again! Yes! I'm UNSTUCK, free, and advancing in you. I AM BECOMING! In Jesus' name!

James 2:14-26, Hebrews 4:1-14, Isaiah 43:18-19, 2 Corinthians 5:7, Hebrews 12:1-2

_____

_____

_____

_____

_____

YOU SUPPLY EVERYTHING

*My connection to you is the power behind all my
thoughts, actions, and efforts to produce.*

Father, I say, I'm connected to you, and I acknowledge that YOU SUPPLY EVERYTHING I need to fulfill my destiny and become me! My connection to you is the power behind all my thoughts, actions, and efforts to produce. I reject deceptive voices that try to tell me I can do things on my own. I won't allow "busy" to get mistaken for faith-driven "productive actions" which produce measurable results. You demonstrated the pattern of how to use faith when you created this world— faith drives my words and every action to produce order and bring light to my day. I AM BECOMING! In Jesus' name!

James 2:14-26, John 15:1-8, Matthew 7:21-23, Genesis 1:1

_____

_____

_____

_____

_____

_____

RELENTLESS COMPASSION

Help me to embrace every opportunity
to be a reflection of your unfailing love.

Father, I say, I will show RELENTLESS COMPASSION towards everyone I encounter today. Your love is never failing towards me, so I refuse to allow past hurt, offense, or any other dysfunctional experiences, to shape or limit how I love, live, and give today. As I create goals and execute plans, help me to embrace every opportunity, to be a reflection of your unfailing love. Let the kind words, smiles, compliments, and other acts of kindness, which I will purposely sow today, open the hearts of others to see you. I AM BECOMING! In Jesus' name!

Psalm 36:5-7, Proverbs 16:9,   2 Corinthians 1:3-5

_____

_____

_____

_____

_____

_____

PERFORMANCE-BASED RIGHTEOUSNESS

Your gift of righteousness permits me to LIVE free from worry and fear as I grow, develop, and overcome.

Father, I say, worry and fear are the off springs of an incorrect, and often hidden belief in PERFORMANCE-BASED RIGHTEOUSNESS. I reject the lie that "Since I created my problems, I have to fix them." Father, you know the good, bad, and the ugly about me, yet you accept me while my mind is renewed, and I'm forever being transformed. Challenges will come, whether I created them, or others caused them. But I choose to believe and stop worrying! I understand that your acceptance of me is not a "free pass" from responsibility. Reading, believing, and applying Your Word are the keys to my walking by faith. Your gift of righteousness permits me to LIVE free from worry and fear, as I grow, develop, and overcome. I AM BECOMING! In Jesus' name!

Matthew 6:25-27, Romans 12:2, 2 Corinthians 5:21, Luke 15:11-32

_____

_____

_____

_____

I KNOW

As the roots of my awareness spread deeper into your love,
my foundation grows stronger.

Father, I say, thank you for calling and equipping me to do everything my destiny requires. Thank you for giving me Jesus as an example of how to respond to the seductive and often tempting voice of the Enemy. It seems to get louder and more frequent the more I advance and make progress into the higher levels of my calling. So, even though I may hear the Enemy, I KNOW your voice! As the roots of my awareness spread deeper into your love, my foundation grows stronger. I AM BECOMING! In Jesus' name!

Hebrews 13:20-21, Matthew 4:1-11, Colossians 2:6-7,
Ephesians 3:16-21, John 10:1-18

_____

_____

_____

_____

_____

_____

A PROBLEM DEFINED

A problem defined, is a problem that can be solved.

Father, I say, a PROBLEM DEFINED is a problem that can be solved. I thank you that I'm not distracted by interruptions, illusions, and the counterfeit decoys of the Enemy. Allow me to hear, think about, and see everything I face through the eyes of faith. By faith, I will speak to all mountains using your Word. I believe that change is imminent! Thank you in advance for giving me a clear vision and the courage to identify, prioritize, boldly attack, and solve real problems today. Seeking you remains my highest priority. I AM BECOMING! In Jesus' name!

Acts 6: 1-7, Mark 11:22-24

_____

_____

_____

_____

_____

_____

DISCIPLINE

*One second of discipline yields far more
fruit than one second of regret.*

Father, I say, You are my shield, my help, and my hope. Your unlimited love energizes and encourages me. My birth and Your remarkable gift of life started the journey of me becoming me. Reaching my full potential is my goal. Today I embrace the power of Christ's victory on the cross, that brought me into good standing with you., It also keeps me being me! As I go through my day today, I will remember, that one second of DISCIPLINE yields far more fruit, than one second of regret, which breeds stagnation. I am progressing, achieving, and I AM BECOMING! In Jesus' name!

*Psalm 33:20-22, Ecclesiastes 7:8, Hebrews 12:11 (MSG),
Philippians 3:12-16, 1 Peter 3:18*

_____

_____

_____

_____

_____

_____

DRAWING NEAR

I start my day by once again, making you the center of my focus.

Father, I say, I'm not always given the opportunity to pick or choose the type or timing of the challenges I encounter. Today I start my day by once again, making you the center of my focus. I seek after, you and give you my attention first! I will not allow any known or newly encountered giants, to distract me from acknowledging and DRAWING NEAR to You, and Your amazing love for me! What grants me the audacity to approach you, whether I caused the problem, or it came upon me? Jesus Christ is the answer! I accept and acknowledge that He alone allows me to enter into Your mercy and grace whenever I need you. Thank you, Father! I AM BECOMING! In Jesus' name!

1 Samuel 4-11, Matthew 6:33, James 4:8-10, Hebrews 4:14-16, John 1:14

_____

_____

_____

_____

_____

_____

WHAT IF? (Part #1)

I'll spend my first 5-10 minutes in your Word,
before I start my day today.

Father, I say, today, I'll use the gifts of imagination and creativity to add more hours to my day. WHAT IF today, I acted as if there was no right or wrong way to approach you, and ignored religious protocol designed to "get me right," before I talked to you? WHAT IF I spent just 5-10 minutes in your Word or on a devotion to start my day? WHAT IF I prayed or praised during my shower? WHAT IF I listened to the digital bible, or a sermon during my morning commute? I would create time, dedicated to taking me deeper into you, and closer to my destiny! I AM BECOMING! In Jesus' name!

Ephesians 3:20, Galatians 5:13, Matthew 18:3

_____

_____

_____

_____

_____

_____

WHAT IF? (Part #2)

I'll use Your gifts of imagination and creativity,
to add hours to my day.

Father, I say, today, I'll use Your gifts of imagination and creativity to add more hours to my day. WHAT IF I talked to you silently under my breath, and consciously thought about you, repeatedly throughout my day, to say thank you, telling you I love you, and ask questions and share problems? WHAT IF I read scriptures or reviewed my devotion for a few minutes, on my phone or tablet during lunch or breaks? WHAT IF I became the lead praise singer in my car, as I worship you on my way home? I would create time, dedicated to taking me deeper into you, and closer to my destiny! I AM BECOMING! In Jesus' name!

Romans 10:17, Luke 6:38, Psalm 86:12

_____

_____

_____

_____

_____

_____

LISTENING, LOOKING & SPEAKING (Part #1)

Whether I chose my giants, or my giants chose me,
I'll speak to them in faith.

Father, I say, forgive me for just LISTENING to my giants, LOOKING at my mountains, and not consistently SPEAKING to them both! If I've lacked or had limited fruit, in any area of my life, it's because I stopped speaking your Words of faith! Your Word continually renews my mind. My "vocabulary of faith words" is steadily increasing! Just as a parent talks to a child, I imagine you saying to me, "Use your words—use your faith words!" So right now, Father regardless of whether I chose my giants, or my giants chose me, I speak in faith, and I am advancing! I AM BECOMING! In Jesus' name!

Mark 11:12-26, Proverbs 13:2-4, Romans 12:2

_____

_____

_____

_____

_____

_____

LISTENING, LOOKING & SPEAKING (Part #2)

Thank you for allowing me to look at giants through your eyes and to see them as you do.

Father, I say, forgive me for just LISTENING to my giants, LOOKING at my mountains, and for not consistently SPEAKING to them both! I thank you for the discernment and wisdom to recognize giants before they grow up! However, I realize it takes only one stone, propelled by Your Word, coming out of my mouth, and guided by Your hand, to open the door to my victory! I won't face giants in my strength and abilities, but I'll yield my natural ability to your supernatural power! You have equipped me to fight, but I realize that the battle is yours and has already been won! Thank you for allowing me to look at giants through your eyes, and to see them as you do. I am advancing, and I AM BECOMING! In Jesus' name!

Mark 11:12-26, 1 Samuel 17:23, 1 Samuel 17:32,37, 1 Samuel 17:45-48, Proverbs 16:9 MSG

_____

_____

_____

_____

_____

REROUTING

*I'll quiet myself to listen to your voice
to guide and direct my focus.*

Father, I say, although I may start my day with plans, schedules, and to-do's, I quiet myself now, to listen to your voice while seeking guidance and direction, to calibrate my focus. Your will for me is my greatest desire. You know every aspect of my life, so I trust you to REROUTE me as needed, so I can dominate my day! Your direction not only allows my daily needs to be met, but I thank you that I will lack nothing in any aspect of my life! As you lead me, I will avoid danger, decrease, or eliminate unneeded effort, successfully navigate detours, and identify places of provision. Thank you, Father! I AM BECOMING! In Jesus' name!

Proverbs 16:9, Matthew 16:24, Psalm 139:1-6, Matthew 2:12-15, Matthew 2:19-20, Joshua 1:1-9

_____

_____

_____

_____

_____

STOP STRIVING

I embrace my relationship with you,
as the only way for me to discover who I am.

Father, I say, thank you for accepting me now, and during every stage of my growth and development in you. I once believed that my accomplishments in my vocation, finances, wealth, education, marital status, and other relationships defined me. Ambition, focus, drive, and determination were my primary tools. I now embrace my relationship with you, as the only way for me to discover who I am. I STOPPED STRIVING, and entered into your love and rest. You are the only way for me to become who I am destined to be! In you, I AM BECOMING! In Jesus' name!

Luke 13:24, Psalm 46:10, Psalm 23:6

_____

_____

_____

_____

_____

_____

SUPERNATURAL FAITH

My life is a conduit to bring unseen imaginations
and desires into the seen.

Father, I say, my faith in the natural world is limited to what I can see, feel, hear, taste, and smell. However, your SUPERNATURAL FAITH is a gift, given to me as a fruit of Your Holy Spirit, when I first believed in Your Son. I am excited that I did not receive "little faith" or "great faith," but rather a faith I can grow and expand, as I read and meditate on your Word. My mind is renewed, my belief is expanded, and my life becomes a conduit to bring unseen imaginations and desires into the seen. Thank you for the gift of faith! I AM BECOMING! In Jesus' name!

Ephesians 2:8, Romans 12:3, Galatians 5:22-23, Matthew 8:10, 26, Romans 4:17, Romans 10:17, Galatians 2:20

_____

_____

_____

_____

_____

_____

TASTE AND SEE

*An inner transformation allows me to see and experience
the manifestation of Your goodness in my life!*

Father, I say, I normally see things, before I taste, eat, then digest them, to gain nourishment and strength. As I daily consume the water, milk, and meat of your Word, the seen is being birthed from the unseen! I'm being changed from the inside out! This inner transformation drives my change, attracts resources, repels enemies, ultimately allowing me to see and experience, the manifestation of Your goodness in my life! You allow me to TASTE AND SEE! Your Goodness, Love, Wisdom, and Word are amazing! Thank you, Father! I AM BECOMING! In Jesus' name!

*Ephesians 5:26, John 4:10-14, 1 Corinthians 3:2, Hebrews 5:12-13,
1 Peter 2:2-3, Ephesians 1:17-19, Psalm 119:103, Psalm 34:8*

_____

_____

_____

_____

_____

_____

THAT'S FOOLISH

It's You who gives me the strength to do and become,
especially when and where I'm weak.

Father, I say, thank you that my education, personality, relationships, and life experiences do not determine my transformation into your image. Nothing except my heart surrendered to you qualifies me to become like, and to be used by you. Some might say THAT'S FOOLISH! I KNOW that you embrace me, right where I am. You allow me to use what I have, while I'm changing, growing, and discovering. Amazing! Though I may excel in some areas more than others, you give me the strength to do and become, especially when and where I'm weak. Thank you, Father! I can only become me in You. I AM BECOMING! In Jesus' name!

2 Corinthians 3:17-18, Acts 1:8, 1 Corinthians 1:18-30,
2 Corinthians 12:10

_____

_____

_____

_____

_____

THE OUTSIDE

Today, I choose to look at myself and others through your eyes.

Father, I say, today, I choose to look at myself and others through your eyes. Your incomprehensible love knows everything about me, yet because of my belief in your Son, you only see me as righteous. Let your love flow freely through me, as I interact with others. Allow me to look past whatever I see on THE OUTSIDE, and use me to touch their hearts, with Your love. I desire to judge not. You are my example! I AM BECOMING! In Jesus' name!

Mark 12:29-31, 2 Corinthians 5:21, 1 Samuel 16:7, Romans 14:1-13, Luke 6:31-42

_____

_____

_____

_____

_____

_____

_____

WITH ME

I won't stay distracted by the storms of life
which attempt to cloud my view of you.

Father, I say, in everything I think, say, or do, and everywhere I go, you are WITH ME. You are WITH ME during the good times. I also acknowledge your presence when things aren't going according to my plans. I don't believe that challenges or setbacks are permanent, so I won't stay distracted by the storms of life, which attempt to cloud my view of you. I realize that drawing near to you occurs when I acknowledge your presence, especially when things are unclear. Yes, you are always WITH ME, and I choose to think about things that reflect my victory in you! I AM BECOMING! In Jesus' name!

Joshua 1:9, Isaiah 41:10, Romans 8:38-39, James 4:7-8, Philippians 4:4-8

_____

_____

_____

_____

_____

_____

PREPARING FOR THE NEXT LEVEL

*I realize that being diligent with what I have, right where I am,
is a requirement for advancement.*

Father, I say, the fruit of consistent, focused, and deliberate faith-driven belief and actions, are keys to PREPARING FOR THE NEXT LEVEL. I realize that being diligent with what I have right where I am, is a requirement for advancement. As I move towards my destiny, I eagerly await your return, and to eventually join you in glory. In the meantime, I will continue to press! As I go into the new day, week, month, or year, I will look at the impossible, and view the unchangeable, through faith. I'll think of doing things I've never done, going places I've never been, and defying the norms and boundaries established by society, and my past. I won't just make resolutions, set goals, or try to change my behavior. No! I'll keep repeating and restating what you promised in Your Word! I'm standing on the authority you reinstated me into, through Jesus Christ, Your Son! You are with me, I'm transformed! I'm walking in the authority of a believer! Yes! I AM BECOMING! In Jesus' name!

Philippians 3:20, Hebrews 11:1-40, Philippians 3:14

DISCOURAGE

I ENCOURAGE MYSELF

Victories come as you enable me to see things through your eyes.

Father, I say, victory comes when I go through tough times and when I put and keep my eyes on you. I ENCOURAGE MYSELF, not just by my actions, but also by the joy and strength that comes by making you the center of my attention. It's your touch that reassures me in the midst of storms. No, I can't manufacture my victories; they come as you enable me to see things through your eyes, from your perspective— and Oh what a view! Being in your presence allows me to turn down the "volume of distraction," and change the "picture of despair," as you touch me! Your peace, that passes all understanding, continually and consistently inspires me to action! I am encouraged, and I AM BECOMING! In Jesus' name!

Matthew 14:24-32, Mark 11:12-14 ,20-24, 1 Samuel 30:6-8, 16-20, Philippians 4:4-9

_____

_____

_____

_____

_____

I ENCOURAGE OTHERS

My encouraging attitude, and the way I engage my day,
helps to ignite hope.

Father, I say, today my tongue releases life! I ENCOURAGE OTHERS as I think, believe, and speak Your Word. My encouraging attitude, and the way I engage my day, help to ignite hope. I thank you for allowing me to share your light and life, so that others can become inspired, by getting to know you and by experiencing your love. It's an exhilarating process being encouraged, followed by my being empowered to encourage others! The noise of life and distractions of difficulties can't compare to the focus provided by your protection and deliverance. I AM BECOMING! In Jesus' name!

Proverbs 18:21, 1 Samuel 30:6, 1 Thessalonians 5:11, Isaiah 40:31, Isaiah 43:2

_____

_____

_____

_____

_____

_____

SEEDTIME AND HARVEST

Any gift or talent that I sow, is preprogrammed with a purpose!

Father, I say, as I acknowledge and thank you for victories, I realize that any destiny-progress made, is a result of your favor, and a harvest from seeds which were sown by faith, somewhere in my past. While I don't always give to get, I acknowledge that the principle of SEEDTIME AND HARVEST, is forever at work in my life. Whether I sow a friendly smile, an encouraging word, or another gift or talent, each is preprogrammed with purpose! Harvests, no matter how small, are the bricks that pave the road to greater crops and my eventual destiny! I AM BECOMING! In Jesus' name!

Genesis 8:22, Galatians 6:7-10, Luke 6:38, Mark 11:23

_____

_____

_____

_____

_____

_____

FULL

I will continue to put every area of my life
under the control of Your Spirit.

Father, I say thank you that I am FULL of Your Spirit! Your Word
and Your Holy Spirit impact my life, from the inside out! As I grow
in the understanding and application of Your Word, I will continue
to put every area of my life under the guidance of Your Spirit. Like
a well-trained soldier, my actions follow my renewing mind. As I
meditate on Your Word, habitual "self-talk" lifts me and inspires
my faith-filled actions. When issues interrupt my thoughts and
attitudes, my spirit-filled life and renewed mind keep me moving
forward to my destiny. I AM BECOMING! In Jesus' name!

Ephesians 5:18, Luke 6:45 NIV, Colossians 3:16, Romans 8:32,
Mark 5:28–29, Psalm 37:23

_____

_____

_____

_____

_____

_____

DEEPER

As I read and reflect on your Word,
the real me is exposed, renewed, and transformed!

Father, I say that this morning, and as often as needed throughout my day, I will purposely slow down, to reflect on who you are to me. Your Word is so alive, so powerful, and so specific, that as I read and reflect on it, the real me is exposed, renewed, and transformed! Growing DEEPER isn't just activated by my knowledge of your Word or my understanding of you, it comes as I apply your Word to my everyday life and relationships. Right thinking produces the right living and breeds the right relationships. You make my natural—supernatural. I AM BECOMING! In Jesus' name!

Jeremiah 15:16, Hebrews 4:12, Romans 10:17, Luke 8:11, James 1:22

_____

_____

_____

_____

_____

CLEAR CONSCIENCE

Thank you for the freedom to be me in you!

Father, I say, thank you, that my righteousness is not based on my past, present or future performance. Knowing that I am made whole in Jesus Christ, gives me the power to apologize when needed, change my behavior as required, and grow relationships with a CLEAR CONSCIENCE. I refuse to allow guilt, condemnation, and justification by "do's and don'ts," to alter my future outlook and activity. My believing, thinking, and feeling right, is not because of what I do—it's because of you. Thank you for the freedom to be me in you! I AM BECOMING! In Jesus' name!

Roman 4:4-25, Job 27:6, 1 Peter 3:16-22, Acts 24:16

_____

_____

_____

_____

_____

_____

_____

AWARE

I think only about good things, believe, then speak by faith to bring the unseen into the seen.

Father, I say, Your Peace is the compass that gives me confidence to acknowledge, engage, and overcome problems. It allows me to see the seeds of opportunities that are often cloaked by challenges. I'm AWARE of the victories that are often realized by aggressively embracing these opportunities. I won't just see problems; I'll look through them to the prize on the other side. I'm fueled by your promises. I only think about good things, believe, then speak by faith, thereby giving birth of the unseen into the seen. You are my rock! You are my victory! I AM BECOMING! In Jesus' name!

Genesis 41:33-36, 1 Samuel 17:26, Psalm 16:6-11, Numbers 13:30, Philippians 4:8

_____

_____

_____

_____

_____

_____

_____

ALL IN

Unsown seeds never produce harvests.

Father, I say, unsown seeds never produce harvests, so I choose to live my life "ALL IN," today and every day. By faith and with self-discipline, I will timely and creatively sow all of the gifts and talents that I've discovered in myself, to help advance your kingdom. I will relentlessly rediscover, uncover, and stir up additional abilities, that will help to unlock my future. Anything I can do is merely a reflection of your presence and power, being released from the unseen to the seen, through me. I'm just a conduit—You are the power that creates, produces, and multiplies. As I live "ALL IN," I AM BECOMING! In Jesus' name!

Matthew 25:14-30, 2 Timothy 1:6-7, Luke 6:38, Galatians 6:7

_____

_____

_____

_____

_____

_____

ANOTHER TOUCH

Your words are in my mouth,
and they allow me to influence my world!

Father, I say, that being transparent with you opens the door to an intimacy which allows me to share my innermost thoughts and feelings without fear, shame, or regret. This level of intimacy does not reveal anything new to you, because you already know my every thought and desire. Rather, it provides me with the awareness that I am only righteous in you. A touch from you makes me whole and gives me sight. You give me ANOTHER TOUCH as needed, to allow me to continue to see clearly. Your words are in my mouth, and they allow me to influence my world! Finish what you started in me, oh Lord! I AM BECOMING! In Jesus' name!

Mark, 8:22-25, Jeremiah 1:6-10, Psalm 138:8, Luke 6:8

_____

_____

_____

_____

_____

_____

THE FIELDS ARE RIPE

Enable me to see others with your compassion and love today.

Father, I say, I'll start my day today by looking beyond my "to-dos," appointments, and my personal needs. Enable me to see others with your compassion and love today. You bring peace to the hurting, provide answers to the confused, and give life to those who are lost. I could be the answer to someone's prayers today! While my actions or words may help introduce someone to you, I realize many are already experiencing your draw. I may be used as a confirmation of your call, but you bring increase to all! THE FIELDS ARE RIPE with those in need of you. Use me! I AM BECOMING! In Jesus' name!

Matthew 9:35-38, 1 Corinthians 1:24, 1 Corinthians 3:6-9

_____

_____

_____

_____

_____

_____

A STONE'S THROW AWAY

I won't just run towards Giants that may appear,
I will run through them towards my destiny!

Father, I say, no matter what my world looked like when I woke up today, I realize I'm just one act of faith, A STONE'S THROW AWAY, from changing my life forever. I will faithfully sow my natural talents and gifts with the expectation that they will be a vehicle, that delivers your supernatural ability, to shape and change my life and family forever! I won't just run towards Giants that may appear; I will run through them towards my destiny! The battle is yours, Father! I'm just A STONE'S THROW AWAY, from a giant-slaying, life-transforming, destiny-achieving victory. I AM BECOMING! In Jesus' name!

1 Samuel 17:32-51, James 2:14-26

_____

_____

_____

_____

_____

_____

THROUGH ME

I'm being changed and strengthened from the inside out.

Father, I say, by faith, my spirit is made alive and new in you. As I read, embrace, meditate on, and confess your Word, my mind is being renewed. I'm being changed and strengthened from the inside out, as I grow in the revelation, of who I was created to be in you. Although I'm forever grateful to receive Your love, my desire is to be like Your Son Jesus and to give it away freely and unashamedly! As I make progress towards my destiny, don't let the memories of my past failures or hurts, current shortcomings, or ambitions for the future, hinder the flow of Your love THROUGH ME. I give myself away! I AM BECOMING! In Jesus' name!

Ephesians 2:1-10, Romans 12:1-2, Philippians 3:13, 1 John 4:7

_____

_____

_____

_____

_____

_____

_____

I WILL KEEP SPEAKING!

I will maximize every second while I create my faith-driven day!

Father, I say, today, I will have a productive day as I press my thoughts, words, and actions through the gift of faith that you have given me. I embrace the possibilities of my future, while I actively engage in every element of my reality. By faith and with extreme confidence, I'm being transformed, as I follow Your example of how to create and produce. I'll use the dominion you have given me to speak to things. I WILL KEEP SPEAKING until I separate light from darkness, change chaos into order, and create something seen, out of something not seen, in my day, my life, and my world. My focus is not just on having a positive attitude or a "good" day, but rather, to maximize every second while I create my faith-driven day! I AM BECOMING! In Jesus' name!

Romans 12:3, Genesis 1:1-31, Luke 4:1-11, Mark 11:12-14 & 20-24, Mark 11:20-24

_____

_____

_____

_____

HOPE BRINGS JOY

The unseen gives birth to the seen!

Father, I say, Godly HOPE BRINGS JOY. I realize that both are gifts, and are released by my faith-driven thinking and expectations. It's by faith that I've developed a bold and confident expectation to stand on Your Word! You not only will do it, but You've already done everything promised in Your Word! Unseen to seen! Unseen to the seen! The unseen gives birth to the seen! I get it, Dad! Faith, Hope, and Love are decisions I've made based on what I believe and think. Feelings follow thoughts. Mind renewal by your Word is the key! I AM BECOMING! In Jesus' name!

Proverbs 10:28 ESV, Galatians 5:22-23, 2 Corinthians 5:7,
Hebrews 11:6, Psalm 27:14 AMP, 1 Corinthians 13:13, Romans 12:2

_____

_____

_____

_____

_____

_____

TRANSFORMED

I see challenges as opportunities and solutions,
instead of magnifying problems.

Father, I say, it is by your mercy and grace that I'm able to grow my surrendered heart, and present my life to you today. Thank you that your Kingdom will be revealed in my world, as my mind is renewed, and I am TRANSFORMED to reflect you! I thank you that not only are my thoughts focused on things that are excellent and worthy of praise, but that I will see challenges as opportunities, see solutions instead of magnifying problems, and I will see victory, from your perspective. Continually allow me to prove your will. Emotions and feelings come and go, but I desire to walk by faith ,continually, every second of every day. Thank you, Father. I AM BECOMING! In Jesus' name!

Romans 12:1-2 2, Matthew 6:10, Matthew 17:2-6, Philippians 4:8-8, Corinthians 5:7

_____

_____

_____

_____

_____

UNCOVER MY TALENTS!

Help me to uncover talents, my time, and any gifts,
which have been hidden or muted, due to the circumstances of life.

Father, I say, thank you for allowing me to learn and get to know your character and personality, as revealed by Your Word and Your Holy Spirit. All that I have comes from, and belongs to you! I am merely a steward for a season. Thank you for providing the relationships, resources, and opportunities I need, to succeed in every endeavor. Today, I focus on giving, sowing, contributing, and adding value. Once again, I plant the seed of my life into you! As I give today, help me to UNCOVER MY TALENTS, my time, and any gifts which have been hidden, or muted, due to circumstances of life. I thank you in advance for the harvest! I AM BECOMING! In Jesus' name!

Matthew 25:14-30, 1 Corinthians 12:4-7, Luke 6:38, Genesis 8:22

_____

_____

_____

_____

_____

_____

WHAT'S THAT AROMA?

In you, I'm learning to establish what I desire
and eliminate what I despise.

Father, I say, spending time with you in Your Word, shapes my thoughts, words, and actions, while it influences my responses and focus. WHAT'S THAT AROMA? I will maintain an awareness that the fragrance I bear is from being with you! In you, I'm learning to establish what I desire, and eliminate what I despise. I'm on a collision-course with my destiny today, and the "winds of resistance" can't alter my steps. In fact, the opposition only intensifies my dependence upon you, while accelerating my ability to obtain all that you have for me. I AM BECOMING! In Jesus' name!

2 Corinthians 2:14-17, Romans 8:28, 2 Corinthians 12:10,
Ephesians 5:1-2, Genesis 45:4-8

_____

_____

_____

_____

_____

_____

WHEN I DON'T SEE

*Like a farmer, I plant the seeds of my desires
into the soil of the unseen with full expectation of growth.*

Father, I say, I believe by faith, not just when I see, but also WHEN I DON'T SEE. My belief births hope. Like a farmer, I plant the seeds of my desires into the soil of the unseen, with the full expectation that the pre-programmed purpose and harvest will be released. So it is with my destiny. I'm inspired to look with expectancy, adjust, and, if necessary, look again through the same lens of faith. Today, I'm walking by faith, with expectancy, as each revelation, each idea, each skill, each relationship, and each destiny-step is being planted, formed, or released! I AM BECOMING! In Jesus' name!

2 Corinthians 5:7, 1 Kings 18:43-44, 1 Corinthians 13:13, Mark 4:26-29

_____

_____

_____

_____

_____

_____

_____

UNDER ARREST!

I'm not only standing and walking by faith,
I run with endurance!

Father, I say, as I renew my mind by reading, reflecting on, believing in, and acting on Your Word, it answers all of my questions! Just like a child learning to walk, I realize that I may sometimes fall. When this happens, unjustified, subtle, deceptive, and accusing thoughts arise, which contradict your perception of me. I put those thoughts UNDER ARREST, and bring them in line with Your Word, which picks me back up! I am who You say I am in You! I'm not only standing and walking by faith, but I run with endurance! I AM BECOMING! In Jesus' name!

Proverbs 24:16, Ephesians 6:13-18, 2 Corinthians 10:5, Hebrews 12:1

_____

_____

_____

_____

_____

_____

DERAIL

I CAN, I WILL, BECAUSE HE DID!

Doing "my all" to stand is not a reflection of my abilities, but rather, it stems from my total and continual faith and reliance in Jesus!

Father, I say, today as I focus on converting my personal desires and latent potential into tangible accomplishments, I'll adapt your perspective of any resistance I encounter. Doing "my all" to stand does not reflect my abilities, but rather it stems from my total and continual faith and reliance on Jesus! I thank you for giving me the strength of your might, the use of your weapons, and the instructions for fighting in a battle that you've already won! I CAN, I WILL, BECAUSE HE DID! I AM BECOMING! In Jesus' name!

Ephesians 6:10-13, 2 Timothy 1:7 NLT, Proverbs 25:28 NLT, Hebrews 12:11-13 NLT, Galatians 5:22-23 NLT, Philippians 4:8 ESV

_____

_____

_____

_____

_____

_____

AT THE TABLE

I fight from a position of strength —
the victory is yours and has already been won.

Father, I say, in the midst of whatever I encounter as I step out and walk by faith today, I am comforted by your goodness and loving-kindness that relentlessly pursues me! My tongue positions me to feast AT THE TABLE you have prepared for me. Victory may not require me to change locations, vocations, or shrink my expectations. I'm expanding my hope, desires, and planning, not only for victory, but also growth! I fight from a position of strength— the victory is yours and has already been won. The good fight of faith I fight—is to keep believing with unwavering conviction. Whether it is people, circumstances, my flesh, my thoughts, or Satan himself that tries to wear me down with opposition, I shall win, and be satisfied with the fruit produced by Your Words, coming out of my mouth. What, me fail? No! Satan is already defeated! God is exalted! Jesus is Lord! I AM BECOMING! In Jesus' name!

Psalm 23, Proverbs 18:20-21, 2 Chronicles 20:15, Isaiah 54:2-3,
1 Timothy 6:12

_____

_____

_____

RENEWED

*I will see challenges as opportunities, and solutions
instead of magnifying problems.*

Father, I say, thank you that your Kingdom will be revealed in my
world today, and that my mind is continually being RENEWED to
reflect you! I thank you that not only are my thoughts focused on
things that are excellent and worthy of praise, but that I will see
challenges as opportunities, see solutions instead of magnifying
problems, and see victory, from your perspective. Allow me to
continually showcase your will. Emotions and feelings come and
go, but I desire to walk by faith, every second of every day. Thank
you, Father. I AM BECOMING! In Jesus' name!

*Matthew 6:10, Romans 12:2, Matthew 17:2-6, Philippians 4:8-8,
2 Corinthians 5:7*

_____

_____

_____

_____

_____

_____

NEVERTHELESS

I have victory in you. I have already won!

Father, I say, I accept and embrace your love, peace, favor, and provision today. As I engage my day, I realize that the perspective of resistance I encounter as I press forward, is determined by how I believe and choose to act. As I follow your voice, I may not fully understand the benefit of your direction. NEVERTHELESS, I'll do what you instruct me to do. Today I will shift my focus from just thinking I merely have an opportunity to win, to believing that I have victory in You! I have already won! I AM BECOMING! In Jesus' name!

Numbers 13:27-30, Luke 5:1-11, Hebrews 11:6, Hebrews 11:1,
1 Corinthians 9:24

_____

_____

_____

_____

_____

_____

_____

HE DID, SO I CAN

I view the difficult, or impossible, *as possible,*
by looking through my eyes of faith.

Father, I say, today, as I reflect on past failures, missed opportunities, or unfulfilled aspirations and desires, I recognize that my focus needs to shift. While reflection is necessary and planning is very helpful, I understand, that to run an efficient race, I must constantly look to your Son Jesus, and keep my eyes forward. As I do so, I will remember and appreciate past favor, successes, and blessings, while believing that the difficult or *impossible*, is possible through the eyes of faith! Everything is working together for my benefit, and the victory of Jesus has already freed me to become! HE DID, SO I CAN! I AM BECOMING! In Jesus' name!

Colossians 1:15-18, Romans 8:28, Hebrews 12:1-2, John 14:12

_____

_____

_____

_____

_____

_____

FAITH SPEAKS!

*Your Word gives life to the pre-programmed purpose
of everything in me!*

Father, I say, as I stand on the truth, that You created and gave life to everything, I am excited that Your Spirit resides in me. When a seed is locked away in the darkness of the soil, water activates its latent potential. So too, does Your Word give life to the pre-programmed purpose of everything in me! I won't confuse talking about things, ideas, or situations, with speaking to them. No, I believe. Therefore FAITH SPEAKS! With deliberate, focused, specific, and precise words, fruit is produced as I speak and work! Today is a new day, and I AM BECOMING! In Jesus' name!

*John 1:1-5, Mark 11:22-25, Numbers 23:19, Isaiah 55:10-11,
Galatians 5:25, James 2:17, Romans 10:17*

_____

_____

_____

_____

_____

_____

COMING OUT!

I realize that "being slow to speak," does not mean to be silent.

Father, I say, thank you for making me whole and new in you. As I engage my day, let my love for you be evident in everything I say and do. While I strive to continue to listen first, I realize that "being slow to speak," does not mean being silent. So I proclaim that I'm COMING OUT of timidity, fear, and false humility today! I'm aware of the world's volatile social climate, but I refuse to feel "wrong," about being made right in you! I openly embrace life and will boldly share my love for you, as I bring your light into this dark world. I AM BECOMING! In Jesus' name!

2 Corinthians 5:17-21, Ephesians 2:8-10, James 1:19,2 Timothy 1:7-10, Matthew 5:10-16

_____

_____

_____

_____

_____

_____

COUNTERFEIT LOVE

Thank you for continuing to show me how to love, accept, and appreciate both the believers and the lost.

Father, I say, I love you! As I continue to experience Your love, I am changing, growing, and learning to love myself. Not because of anything I did or will ever do, but because of you! Just knowing that you have chosen to take up residence in me, gives me the capacity to love others. Life without you is empty. I was once a casualty of COUNTERFEIT LOVE and misplaced affections. Continue to show me how to love, accept, and appreciate both the believers, and the lost who have yet to experience your touch. Allow me to demonstrate a life full of joy and meaning as I become me. Yes, I AM BECOMING! In Jesus' name!

Mark 12:30-31, Romans 13:8-14, 1 Corinthians 3:16, 1 Samuel 16:7, Ecclesiastes 1:2-11

_____

_____

_____

_____

_____

BEING UNIQUELY ME

Thank you for giving me creative ways to demonstrate your love
by being uniquely me

Father, I say, today, I will not allow the needle of my life, to slip back into the groove of a "normal" routine. My purpose today is to play louder or, if needed, a different tune. By faith, my actions will demonstrate my reconnection to you through Jesus, your Son. I am excited about BEING UNIQUELY ME. I am an empowered representative of Heaven, a passionate lover and provider for my family, and an uncommon producer in my calling. Thank you for giving me creative ways to demonstrate your love, by BEING UNIQUELY ME today. People will be impacted by, and drawn to Your Spirit in Me. I AM BECOMING! In Jesus' name!

Matthew 28:19, James 2:17, 1 John 5:7-15, Philippians 3:14

_____

_____

_____

_____

_____

_____

IT IS GOOD!

One way for me to touch my tomorrow,
is to live completely today.

Father, I say, I begin my day with faith-filled words of creation. If I don't complete every task or reach every goal, I'll reflect on the progress I've made, and acknowledge that IT IS GOOD! I'll seek you first, while I accomplish what I can, with what I have. I thank you for any new ideas, resources, or relationships I develop today, which will help me. My focus is on the now, and I realize that one way for me to touch my tomorrow, is to live completely today. It's you who give me the grace and power to start and finish! I'm producing, I'm finishing, and I AM BECOMING! In Jesus' name!

Genesis 1:1-31, Matthew 6:25-34 (MSG), Matthew 25:14-21,
Matthew 6:11, Zechariah 4:6

_____

_____

_____

_____

_____

_____

ABSENT OF DISTRACTIONS

Emotions and feelings pass, but I desire to walk by faith,
every second, of every day.

Father, I say, the breath of life that you breathed into man at creation, is what allows me to continue experiencing your Presence. Yes, I am Your vessel, and I thank you for living and residing in me. Thank you for promising never to leave me, even when I sometimes fail to acknowledge you, because of the noise of life. Father, I desire to recognize and be conscious of your Presence, every second, of every day. I realize that a pure heart is not defined by the absence of ungodly desires or misplaced aspirations, but rather by a heart ABSENT OF DISTRACTIONS. Emotions and feelings pass, but I desire to walk by faith, every second, of every day. I realize that I can only become me—IN YOU. Thank you, Father. I AM BECOMING! In Jesus' name!

Genesis 2:7, Proverbs 20:27, Hebrews 13:5, 2 Corinthians 5:7

_____

_____

_____

_____

_____

DETOURS

Faith in your Word puts, and keeps me,
on the main road to my destiny.

Father, I say, today I choose to focus on you, even when everyday life or the Enemy presents me with DETOURS. Whether my focus is being interrupted by family, friends, or other relationships, health-related challenges, finances, or my career, I thank you for the power of your Word, and the leading of the Holy Spirit, which empowers me to speak to them! I speak peace and calmness to chaos and storms, light to any darkness, and healing to ANY sickness or disease. Faith in your Word puts and keeps me, on the main road to my destiny. I AM BECOMING! In Jesus' name!

Proverbs 18:21, Genesis 1:2-3, Luke 10:38-42, Mark 4:39,
Matthew 6:24-34, 3 John 1:2

_____

_____

_____

_____

_____

_____

ILLUSIONS OF SUCCESS

Allow my desires, and the things I say,
to continually line-up with Your purpose,
as You establish my every step.

Father, I say, today I won't be drawn off by the counterfeit ILLUSIONS OF SUCCESS that are designed to distract, delay, and ultimately destroy my destiny. My attention will remain focused on my submission and obedience to Your Word, and Your voice. Allow my desires and the things I say, to continually line-up with Your purpose, as You establish my every step. I won't question my identity, or get tricked into compromising my worship of you, to try to acquire provisions or reach goals of things you've already promised! I refuse to allow fear to influence or break my focus. No Fear! No Fear! No Fear! I AM BECOMING! In Jesus' name!

3 John 1:2, 1 Samuel 15:9-28, Proverbs 14:18-28 (MSG),
Matthew 4:8-11, 1 John 5:13-15 (MSG), Proverbs 16:9, Proverbs 19:21,
1 Corinthians 13:11-12

_____

_____

_____

_____

ISSUES OF LIFE

I quiet myself now and welcome your words, your touch,
and acknowledge your never-ending presence.

Father, I say, when I draw near to you, there have been times when I haven't sensed your movement towards me, or noticed an increase in your presence. In fact, I've asked myself the question, "What's wrong with me?" Thank you for lovingly revealing, that when I don't sense you, it's not because you've left me for any reason, but rather, it's when I've allowed the ISSUES OF LIFE to speak louder to me than your voice. I quiet myself now, welcome your words and touch, and acknowledge your never-ending presence. I thank you for never leaving me. I AM BECOMING! In Jesus' name!

Jeremiah 29:13-14 (MSG), James 1:3-4, James 4:8

_____

_____

_____

_____

_____

_____

NEED-TO-KNOW

I'll lean on and trust in Your Words,
and make them the basis for what I speak.

Father, I say, thank you for revealing the hidden agendas and details that I NEED TO KNOW about the people, places, and things I will encounter in my life today. This revelation will show me whom to celebrate, what to avoid, and how to speak. I'll lean on and trust in Your Words, and make them the basis for what I speak to create, shape, direct, and transform my day. Thanks for keeping me on a NEED-TO -KNOW basis so that I'll remain focused on you! I AM BECOMING! In Jesus' name!

Proverbs 3:5-6, Psalm 37:23, Daniel 2:22, Proverbs 18:21

_____

_____

_____

_____

_____

_____

_____

TEMPTATION IS NOT A SIN!

*The freedom I have in Jesus, allows me to keep it real,
and to have full transparency with you.*

Father, I say, thank you for your Word and the leadings of Your Holy Spirit, who prepares me for the thoughts, sights, feelings, and other temptations, which may come to me throughout my day today. Your Word tells me there will always be temptations, so today, I expose the Enemy, who is the Tempter and Accuser. He speaks, to try to break my focus, and slow or stop my forward progress. But Your Kingdom is forever advancing! To silence his voice, I recognize, proclaim, and walk guilt-free with you, as I advance! TEMPTATION IS NOT A SIN! The freedom I have in Jesus, allows me to keep it real, and to have full transparency of all my thoughts and feelings. Father, I love talking with You! I AM BECOMING! In Jesus' name!

*Matthew 4:3, Revelation 12:10, Luke 17:1, Luke 22:40,
1 Corinthians 10:13*

_____

_____

_____

_____

TUG-OF-WAR

I freely make you the center of my unbroken focus.

Father, I say, thank you for allowing me to win the TUG-OF-WAR that many wish they could ignore. I've learned that—whatever has my attention, will control me—so I freely make you the center of my unbroken focus. As I embrace your Word, and follow Your voice, the changing and molding that happens, fuels advancement toward my desires and destiny. I thank you, for bringing me from where I was, and I'm truly excited about where you are taking me! Life in your Spirit is amazing! I AM BECOMING! In Jesus' name!

Romans 7:21-25, 2 Corinthians 6:14-18, Romans 8:1-12, Matthew 6:33

_____

_____

_____

_____

_____

_____

_____

YOUR WORD AND YOUR WILL

Decisions eliminate options and give birth to self-discipline!

Father, I say, by faith, I'm standing, and believing for, (*fill-in-your-request*).   As I fight "the good fight" of faith, I stand and choose to speak Your Word, with the hope I will possess what I through faith confess. Doubt and the thought of failure may occasionally come to mind. But I thank You for giving me Your Word to knock down the lie, that I've "wavered," because of a passing negative thought or feeling. No, I'm not moved by them! I'll continually say "yes" to YOUR WORD AND YOUR WILL. I believe by faith, and trust in you with all of my heart!   Decisions eliminate options and give birth to self-discipline! I AM BECOMING! In Jesus' name!

1 Timothy 6:12, 2 Corinthians 4:13, 2 Timothy 1:7, Proverbs 3:5-6, James 1:6-7, 2 Corinthians 10:5, Daniel 1:8, Daniel 6:10

_____

_____

_____

_____

_____

DISCREDIT

DEAD FAITH

I won't confuse the "busyness of life,"
with correctly applied, faith-driven, "productive activities."

Father, I say, today I won't have DEAD FAITH. My connection to you supplies everything I need to conquer this day, fulfill my destiny, and become me! I reject deceptive thoughts and voices that tell me I can accomplish life's objectives without you. You gave me the power to create and produce, and I realize my *actions* complete my faith. I won't confuse the "busyness of life" with correctly applied, faith-driven, "productive activities." I won't move, and then try to apply faith to my efforts. Faith will drive my every *action!* I AM BECOMING! In Jesus' name!

James 2:14-26, John 15:1-8, Matthew 7:21-23, Genesis 1:1

_____

_____

_____

_____

_____

_____

REMEMBERED, BUT NOT RELIVED

*Bad memories won't determine my future, or my destiny,
because I'm new in you!*

Father, I say, physical or mental scars from painful interactions with anyone, including strangers, acquaintances, friends, a spouse, or blood relatives, will no longer affect my future! Negative things are REMEMBERED, BUT NOT RELIVED. Bad memories won't determine my future or my destiny, because I'm new in you! I realize that shame, and hurt, function as the soil to hide shortcomings. However, new levels of transparency with others are birthed from my transparency with you. My love for you, followed by loving myself, allows me to truly love others. I AM BECOMING! In Jesus' name!

2 Corinthians 5:17, Colossians 3:1-15, Mark 12:30-31

_____

_____

_____

_____

_____

_____

MEMORIES

Thank you for creating me in your image,
and for making me a reflection of you.

Father, I say, thank you for creating me in your image, and making me a reflection of you. You created everything. You love me so much, that you've given me the authority, and ability, to contribute to the future creation-process. The gift of memory allows me to re-play what you want me to remember from my past. I especially thank you, for the precious MEMORIES of all the good times and experiences I was blessed to have, with family and friends. Your unique gifts of imagination and creativity allows me by faith, to pre-play, speak to, and create my future! I AM BECOMING! In Jesus' name!

Genesis 1:26-27, Genesis 2:19, Psalm 8:3-9, Ephesians 3:20,
Philippians 3:12-16, Philippians 4:8

_____

_____

_____

_____

_____

IT TAKES ONLY ONE THOUGHT!

Right thinking is what propels me to a life of victory.

Father, I say, wrong thinking forms chains that hold me back from maximizing my life. Right thinking is what propels me to a life of victory. I choose to think correctly about who I am in Christ, and to believe Your Word, to drive my actions today! I arise now with boldness, confidence, eagerly awaiting, always anticipating, and believing that I'm well-able! IT TAKES ONLY ONE THOUGHT, followed by another, then another, and another, to accomplish what you want me to do! Consuming, digesting, believing, and embracing Your Word is the key! I am becoming! Yes, I AM BECOMING! In Jesus' name!

Psalm 107:13-16, Philippians 4:6-7, 2 Corinthians 4:3-4, Proverbs 28:1, 2 Corinthians 3:11-12, Numbers 13:30

_____

_____

_____

_____

_____

_____

I SEE IT!

I won't decide who's in my inner circle,
I will discern it, by Your Spirit!

Father, I say, I will lovingly, keenly, and freely engage with people today. I will wisely discern and sow the seeds I am assigned to plant into their lives and futures. Whether I'm to sow my gifts and talents, provide a service, or give of my substance, open my eyes and heart, so I SEE IT! Similarly, I pray that those who are called to be a part of my destiny, will come into my world, while you reveal to me, those who I am to exclude. I won't decide who's my inner circle, I will discern it, by Your Spirit! I AM BECOMING! In Jesus' name!

Matthew 6:1-4, 2 Corinthians 9:6-7, Matthew 26:17-25

_____

_____

_____

_____

_____

_____

FREEDOM

You direct me as I walk, encourage me to run,
and pick me up, if ever I fall.

Father, I say, thank you for a new morning of miracles, and another day of victory! As I learn more and more about how you've equipped me, I get a clearer picture of who I am in you. I embrace my FREEDOM to live, change, move, and grow in You. It's exciting! You direct me as I walk, encourage me to run, and pick me up, if I ever fall. I receive dominion, Father! Thank you! I AM BECOMING! In Jesus' name!

Psalm 8:3-9, Psalm 119:45, John 8:32, 2 Corinthians 3:17,
Galatians 5:1, Luke 4:18

_____

_____

_____

_____

_____

_____

AT THE END OF ME

The key to unlocking the intents and desires that you inspired in my life,
is faith and confidence in you.

Father, I say, the journey to achieve the fullness of the desires, dreams, and ultimately the destiny you've birthed in my heart, is accelerated when I reach THE END OF ME. I refuse to be a public success, yet a private failure. I acknowledge, I can do nothing apart from you. I embrace the end of my false humility, insincere praise, and selfish ambitions. Today my focus is on sharing your love with others. The key to unlocking the intents and desires you inspired in my life, is faith and confidence in you. I AM BECOMING! In Jesus' name!

John 15:5, Luke 9:23-27, 1 Corinthians 4:1-5, Philippians 2:1-4 MSG,
Joel 2:25, 2 Corinthians 12:10

_____

_____

_____

_____

_____

_____

PROSPER

Before my birth, your blessings started forever chasing me!

Father, I say, before I was born, you not only knew everything about me, but you also made provisions for all the plans of my life —my destiny. Before my birth, your blessings started forever chasing me! Unlike the old covenant, which required me to "do," to "qualify" for your blessings, Jesus Christ Your Son, fulfilled every requirement of the law. Now, by faithful "belief" and Your acceptance, I've received the benefits as if I'd obeyed every aspect of your law. Now, not only am I chased by your provision, but I'm also overtaken by everything I need to PROSPER! My health, family, relationships, and finances are whole! I AM BECOMING! In Jesus' name!

Jeremiah 1:5, Matthew 5:17-18, Deuteronomy 28:1-2, Genesis 26:12-25, Hebrews 8:7-12, 3 John 1:2

_____

_____

_____

_____

_____

_____

DIVINE ACCELERATION

I proclaim that you will convert evil intentions towards me,
into shortcuts to favor!

Father, I say, thank you for working out everything for my good. Although DIVINE ACCELERATION may sometimes require me to experience things I may not understand, I know I win by faith! In fact, "setbacks" are often "setups" in disguise. I proclaim that you will convert evil intentions towards me, into shortcuts to favor! Regardless of the reason, things that were lost or stolen are being restored! Father, I recognize and embrace the fact that my strength to accomplish anything comes from you. I AM BECOMING! In Jesus' name!

Romans 8:28, John 10:10, Proverbs 6:30-31, Genesis 50:20,
1 Kings 19:1-21

_____

_____

_____

_____

_____

_____

FAITH INSPIRED TRANSPARENCY

By faith, I have no shame, guilt, or timidity,
in being completely transparent with you!

Father, I say, I'll live my life from the inside out, today! I realize I'm not perfect, but I'm Yours! This morning, I commit once again to You, the flawed, ever-changing, growing, developing, and learning—me. I take off the mask and clothes I use to cover up, and I openly display my total self. By faith, I have no shame, guilt, or timidity. I'm completely transparent with you! Facades and concealment breed stagnation, while my FAITH INSPIRED TRANSPARENCY ignites the change motivated by you! Your unconditional love excites and empowers me. I'm yours! Help me show a dying world, what life in you looks like! I AM BECOMING! In Jesus' name!

Hebrews 4:13, 2 Corinthians 1:12-14, Colossians 2:10

_____

_____

_____

_____

_____

INHERITANCE

I continually discover new potential
as I learn more about who I am in you.

Father, I say, you are my INHERITANCE! The revelation you created, called, and equipped me for achieving my destiny, is amazing! I continually discover new potential, as I learn more about who I am in you. Your love is ever present in me, and I desire to let it drive everything I do! Allow me today to see myself, my family, and others through your love. Thank you for working out all things past, present, and future, to my good, as I gain a clearer vision of my purpose. I AM BECOMING! In Jesus' name!

Psalm 16:5-6, Ephesians 1:11-17, Galatians 4:4-7, John 13:34-35,
Psalm 119:57-59, Romans 8:28

_____

_____

_____

_____

_____

_____

OUT OF THE STORM!

I hear and know your voice.
I thank you for constantly speaking to me!

Father, I say, I hear and know your voice. I thank you for constantly speaking to me! As I align my plans with those you have for me, I'm able to see clearly and make adjustments as I'm progressing! Your direction saves my life! I also thank you for sending me capable, willing counselors and advisers, who help encourage, guide, direct, and affirm me. I thank you for helping me come OUT OF THE STORM! As I experience your rest, allow me to sow the seed of your peace into others today. I AM BECOMING! In Jesus' name!

Isaiah 30:18-21, Proverbs 4:25-27, Isaiah 30:1, Proverbs 16:9,
Proverbs 15:22, Isaiah 43:2

_____

_____

_____

_____

_____

_____

AUDACIOUS BELIEF

Faith makes my AUDACIOUS BELIEF, make sense!

"Father, I say, Your Word summons faith. Every time I read or listen to it, I am encouraged. Whether I'm doing a general reading, an in-depth topical study, or just reading and quoting specific passages of scripture, Your Word accomplishes everything it needs to do, in me. I use it to shape my personality, relationships, education, habits, and ability to focus the other areas of my life, which make up the "raw materials" of my destiny. Faith makes my AUDACIOUS BELIEF make sense! Thank you! I AM BECOMING! In Jesus' name!

Romans 10:17, Isaiah 55:11, 1 John 5:5, 2 Corinthians 4:18

_____

_____

_____

_____

_____

_____

STAND!

My advancement comes from walking in dominion.
I will not go backwards!

Father, I say, to STAND is "to take up, or stay in, a specified position or condition." I will face today, in faith! As I follow the leading of your Spirit, while I do all I can,, I'll STAND! Your armor, the very presence of my Lord Jesus Christ, is the strength that fuels my determination, discovery, and all my efforts. My advancement comes from walking in dominion. I will not go backwards! I'll face every challenge, trial, or temptation by faith, as I embrace Christ's strength instead of my weakness. I AM BECOMING! In Jesus' name!

Romans 13:14, Ephesians 6:13-20, Luke 4:1-13, 2 Sam. 23:11-12

_____

_____

_____

_____

_____

_____

WHAT I SEE

Every time I read, meditate on, and speak your Word,
I get a clearer image of who I am in you.

Father, I say, Your Word gives me encouragement and stability as it shapes the way I think. Every time I read, meditate on, and speak it, I get a clearer image of who I am in you. I thank You that I'm being transformed into WHAT I SEE, as I discover, and say what You said about me. My self-esteem continually rises as I learn how You see me. I accept how wonderfully you created and equipped me to think, imagine, discover, shape, and create my future. I am nothing in myself, but I'm everything in Christ! I AM BECOMING! In Jesus' name!

John 1:12-13, Romans 15:4, Mark 10:27 (MSG), Psalm 8:4-6,
Psalm 139:14-16 (MSG)

_____

_____

_____

_____

_____

_____

WHO ME?

Whether I am to plant or water the seed of your Word,
I know that it is You, who will make it grow.

Father, I say, thank you for giving me life by your Holy Spirit. As I submit myself to you today, let others see and experience your presence in me. Allow me to discern where and how to express compassion to someone who is interested in, or being drawn to you. Let me follow the example of Jesus, and create "WHO ME?" moments for others, by reaching out to those who feel unworthy. Many feel they are missing something in their lives, while others are desiring a touch and glimpse of you. Whether I am to plant or water the seed of your Word, I know it is You who will make it grow. I AM BECOMING! In Jesus' name!

John 6:44, Romans 12:3-4, 1 Corinthians 3:6-9, Luke 19:2-10

_____

_____

_____

_____

_____

_____

WHY DO I HAVE TO DO THAT?

As my mind is being renewed, my words, and actions,
will reflect your Word.

Father, I say, as "life happens" today, I refuse to have my focus on You broken! I will deliberately and continually adjust my thoughts to remain focused on You, while I actively participate in the advancement of Your Kingdom, by living Your Word. I will repeatedly reject any thoughts which try to get me to question my identity as a believer— especially the pride-based question of, "WHY DO I HAVE TO DO THAT?" I embrace Your Love and Your Words. They are the driving factors behind my motives, attitudes, and plans for today. As my mind is being renewed, my words and actions reflect your Word. From the inside out, I AM BECOMING! In Jesus' name!

Matthew 4:1-11, Philippians 4:8, Proverbs 23:7a, Luke 6:45

_____

_____

_____

_____

_____

PART 3

APPENDIX

Salvation

The following prayer is offered to assist you in restoring and strengthening your connection with God. In the past, people's actions determined their acceptance in God's eyes, but now, through faith in Jesus Christ, our bond with Him is based on our faith, according to Hebrews 8:7-10.

Romans 10:13 NLT

"Everyone who calls on the name of the LORD will be saved."

"Everyone" includes you! You're not required to "get right," do right, or change, to approach God. Believe and come to God FIRST! He will help you change and grow!

Romans 10:9-10 NLT

"If you openly declare that Jesus is Lord and believe in your heart that God raised him from the dead, you will be saved. [10] For it is by believing in your heart that you are made right with God, and it is by openly declaring your faith that you are saved."

SAY IT WITH OUR MOUTHS

Verses 9 and 10 tell us that if we openly declare with our mouths that Jesus is Lord and believe in our hearts that God raised Him from the dead, we *"will be saved."* (Eternal Life with God)

SAY THIS PRAYER OUT LOUD NOW

Dear God, I confess my sins and ask for your forgiveness. I want to be a part of your family. You said in Your Word that I would be saved if I acknowledge Jesus as my Lord and Savior and believe that You raised Him from the dead. Jesus, please come into my heart as my Lord and Savior! Thank You for answering my prayer, saving me, and giving me Eternal Life with You. You live, so I live! Thank you, Father, you are in me! You are working through me! Teach me your way. As I read Your Word, allow me to discover and BECOME who I am called to be. In the name of Jesus Christ, I give you my life, Lord. Amen!

WHAT'S NEXT?

If you prayed this prayer for the first time, I welcome you to the family of God!

Cultivate a personal relationship with Jesus through prayer, studying His Word, and seeking guidance from the Holy Spirit.

Regularly attending a Bible-believing church and connecting with fellow believers enables growth and accountability in the faith community.

Embracing a life of love and service, sharing the good news of salvation, and seeking to live out Christ's teachings become fundamental.

The journey entails continually surrendering to God, allowing His transformative power to mold character, and aligning desires with His will. Seeking to emulate Jesus in every aspect of life, developing virtues, and relying on God's grace and strength will become your ongoing pursuit as a believer.

May you become who you were destined to be as you rediscover the dominion authority granted you in the Kingdom of God!

Let us know if you prayed this prayer for the first time or recommitted to a life of faith by visiting *IABCommunity.com/prayer.*

BONUS PREVIEW

*How I used the I AM BECOMING! Program
to develop a unique friendship with Muhammad Ali*

The Bonus Preview excerpts below are taken from a book scheduled to be published in the near future. The book tells how I established a personal relationship with the Champ and reveals some of the secrets I learned about leadership, marketing, and sales while studying his life.

From my first visit with the Champ at his home.

THE LIST

It was nearing 11:00 p.m., and I was still sitting in my office, thinking and trying to clear my head before going home. The small Internet company I was running had, earlier that day, failed in our attempt to raise 1 million dollars of Venture Funding. The owner wanted me to stay on as Vice President but with a 50% cut in pay. I think this was just an "easy way" of getting me to resign, which I did.

What was going on? I was trying to live the Word-based principles I was learning in church, reading personal development books, and completing self-paced courses on key subjects—but the results I had hoped for were not being realized.

Before resigning, during a very uncomfortable late-night meeting I had with myself, I compiled the most comprehensive list of my talents and gifts I'd ever noted. To make sure I didn't miss anything, I asked myself and thoroughly answered the following questions:

THE FOUR QUESTIONS
1) What am I good at doing?
2) What do people say I am or would be good doing?
3) What do I have a strong interest in learning or knowing?
4) What things occasionally interest me?

I believed firmly in setting ambitious goals, stretching, and thinking BIG! However, first, I needed to identify and accept everything God had given me. People had always told me I looked like Muhammad Ali, so I put that on my list, too!

As I sat and thought about my employment options, I asked myself, "Am I missing out on a harvest from seeds I'd never sown?" My decision that night—to live my life "All-In" led me to a unique friendship with the Champ, multiple personal visits, and a memorable birthday celebration in Las Vegas nearly a decade later.

ARE YOU MISSING OUT ON A HARVEST, FROM SEEDS YOU'VE NEVER SOWN?

THE CHAMP'S 70th BIRTHDAY PARTY

The minimum-priced tickets of $1,500 per plate to Muhammad Ali's 70th birthday party had sold out unbelievably fast. I'd relentlessly tried to purchase a ticket on every website I'd found online, but none was available! I spent a week searching! Then, during a brief phone conversation with Lonnie, Muhammad's wife, I learned she had already allocated her reserved tickets, too! However, she offered a glimmer of hope by giving me the event coordinator's personal phone number. I thought, "I don't know how it'll happen, but I'm going to Ali's 70th birthday party!"

Soon, however, my bold stance quickly vanished, giving way to bouts of anxiety and frustration.

The Champ and his family were prudently using his status as one of the world's most recognizable and beloved figures to support two important causes: The Cleveland Clinic's Lou Ruvo Center for

183

Brain Health in Las Vegas and the Muhammad Ali Center in the Champ's hometown of Louisville, KY. The event organizers planned to raise money for these causes while jointly celebrating Ali's incredible legacy and 70th birthday.

The party would bring Ali back to where he'd fought seven times, including three heavyweight title defenses. The celebrity crowd was to include sports and entertainment notables and over 2,000 other dignitaries and guests in one of Las Vegas' most incredible nights of philanthropy.

I felt strongly that I should attend. I also wanted to deliver a unique birthday present to the Champ personally. It was an impressive 30 x 40-inch, framed original black and white oils-over-canvas portrait of the Champ throwing a punch, created by artist Robert L. Stampas, Jr.

An act of faith initially brought about my relationship with the Champ. So why would I approach getting a ticket to this once-in-a-lifetime event differently from how I'd followed God's leading, so many times before?

God was in control, just as He was in 2003 when I took my first steps in faith and purposefully began to sow the gift I had of looking like the Champ!

When things are going well, I am guilty of sometimes thinking I'm in control. When things go wrong, I'm quickly reminded this is not true. Trying times have taught me that I'm only in control of how I prepare for what *might* happen—and my response *after* things happen. God controls when things happen. I accept God's timing as perfect, although embracing His direction has not always seemed easy!

FAITH IN ACTION

There were only a few weeks left before the celebration in Vegas. I still didn't have a ticket! How was I feeling? What did I do? No matter what I tried to think about or focus on, I kept experiencing increased anxiety levels. This feeling of "back-against-the-wall hopelessness" was no stranger to me because it's one of the Enemy's favorite tricks. Focusing on select passages of scriptures helped, but negative thoughts and my self-imposed pressures were relentless—until I finally let go and remembered who I am and Who's I am!

Faith is often considered a positive belief in something or someone. But faith, as described in the Word, is a firm confidence that results in *action!* Faith causes a belief that drives *action!* For example, in Hebrews 11:7-36, *action* follows every mention of faith.

So, what were my faith-driven actions? After praying, which I do constantly, I booked my round-trip plane tickets to Vegas on the same flight as several Ali family members. I made reservations at the host hotel, the MGM Grand. Next, my birthday gift for the

Champ was carefully packed by UPS and shipped to the hotel. Then, once again, I dealt with an overwhelming onslaught of negative thoughts, telling me how foolish I was to make plans and incur the involved expenses, all without having a ticket to the event!

PUT UP, BUT DON'T SHUT UP!

Never let the Opposition silence you. To deal with my toxic thoughts, I deployed one of the most lethal weapons in a believer's arsenal—the spoken Word! (Proverbs 18:21) It's one of the principles Ali himself mastered throughout his life—talking about things that do not yet exist as though they already did! (Romans 4:17)

Ali was, arguably, one of the most famous users of "I AM" quotes who ever lived. He creatively spoke them to shape the type of future and life he wanted. "I am the greatest!" "I am the fastest!" "I am the Champ!" "I am pretty!" He masterfully used this strategy by repeating these and other affirmations over and over again, often in the form of memorable poems and rhymes. He believed them, spoke them, and followed them up with *actions!* He produced results! He wouldn't just say, "I'm fast!" Ali would say, "I float like a butterfly, sting like a bee. Your hands can't hit what your eyes can't see!"

He realized that whatever followed the "I AM..." would eventually find him. So, he talked, and talked, and repeated things loud and long until we started repeating them, too! We echoed what he believed—for him! Ali helped people from all walks of life realize that what follows those two simple words, "I AM," can shape the kind of life they'll live. He *believed* and *spoke.* He also followed his words *with focused action!*

Our spoken words plant seeds, and at some point, we will eat the fruit of our harvest! When I understood that, I really started talking!

I first mentioned my plans to my team at work. I informed them I was taking a long weekend to attend Ali's party in Vegas. Then, I started sharing plans with select family and inner-circle friends. Constantly reading, meditating on, and quoting scriptures supported my words and activities.

God accomplishes amazing feats in our lives if and when we believe Him and obediently *move forward with action!* Faith, like a muscle, grows the more we use it!

Since this is just an excerpt from my forthcoming book, let me summarize a few highlights of my trip below.

MY "ALL-IN" WEEKEND IN LAS VEGAS

The Friday afternoon flight to Vegas was fun. But Saturday morning started with my attempt to fix, manage, and control things.

I hailed a cab and spent $60 traveling around Vegas to find the event coordinator. I finally caught up with the contact Lonnie had mentioned—only to discover nothing had changed! She still didn't have any cancellations. The event was completely sold out! I was devastated, but that feeling lessened briefly after I spent a great afternoon meeting and talking with several of Ali's family members and friends.

About two hours before the start of the Gala, I was sitting in one of the hotel cafes enjoying the company of Muhammad Ali, Jr., and two longtime family friends. These friends, like me, had been unsuccessful in getting tickets. After hearing and sharing several great personal stories about our fun times with the Champ, Ali Jr. stood up, stretched, and said he was going to his room to get changed for the evening event. Shortly after he departed, I stood up and made a similar statement. One of the family friends looked at me, puzzled, and asked, "How are you gonna get in, without a ticket?" I answered, "I told you guys, this whole trip is an *act of faith!* I still don't know how I'll get in, but I'm gonna put on my tux and head to the party's entrance door!"

After changing, I mixed and mingled in the entryway of the MGM Grand Garden Arena with hundreds of eager guests and waited for the doors to open. At one point, I had people lining up to take pictures with me because they thought I was a family member due to my strong resemblance to the Champ. While enjoying the excitement, I eventually ran into several Ali family members making their way through the crowd. They invited me to walk with them to enter the Gala via a special V.I.P. entrance.

The parade of sports and entertainment stars who walked the Red Carpet was magical! The official list of those scheduled to attend included Stevie Wonder, Samuel L. Jackson, David Beckham, Larry King, Ken Jeong, Snoop Dogg, LL Cool J, Common, Lenny Kravitz, Anthony Hopkins, John Legend, Haley Reinhart, Raphael Saadiq, Cee Lo, Joe Perry, Slash, Terrence Howard, David Copperfield, Siegfried & Roy, Andre Agassi, Stefanie Graf, Jim Brown, Randy Couture, Brad Garrett, Kelly Rowland, Dave Koz, and more. Several former boxing icons also made their way into the celebration, including Sugar Ray Leonard, Evander Holyfield, Ken Norton, Earnie Shavers, Leon Spinks, Ray "Boom Boom" Mancini, and Tommy "Hitman" Hearns.

As we made our way down the red carpet, cameras flashed as photographers vied for our attention, "Up top please!" "To the right!" "Up top to the left!" "Everybody here, look right here!" "Right here, straight ahead!" I'd never experienced anything like this in my life!

189

We were then escorted to the main entrance, where security was visible and actively checking all badges. I thought my heart was going to jump out of my chest! As we followed our escort, she told security, "These are members of the Ali family." The entrance personnel all warmly greeted us! Long stares, smiles, and even a few handshakes welcomed us into the Gala's electric atmosphere!

Wait! What just happened? I was *inside* the event! The worrying, the self-imposed pressure, the stress, the wasted time, and the cab fare were all for naught! I realized that *God had all this planned* long before I *faithfully* embarked on my trip to Vegas!

I was grateful to have made it into the event, but my conscience prevented me from taking a seat to eat a meal I hadn't purchased. I told the family that I would connect with them later. I turned to walk the venue, take in the room's high-energy yet cozy ambiance, and reflect on the miracle of God's goodness.

As I casually strolled around the perimeter, my strong resemblance to the Champ once again prompted many people to ask if they could take pictures with me. I also met and talked with several notables: Terrence Howard, Ken Norton, George Foreman, Robert Davi, Ne-Yo, and Sugar Ray Leonard. Then it hit me—you don't have to have great talents or gifts to receive a harvest, but you do have to *sow* them for God to multiply and *use* them in His great way!

190

**You don't have to have great talents or gifts
to receive a harvest, but you do have to *sow* them,
for God to multiply and *use* them in His great way!**

Proverbs 18:16

"A man's gift maketh room for him, and bringeth him before great men."

MY BIRTHDAY PRESENT FOR THE CHAMP

The Champ made a brief appearance early Sunday afternoon to greet the people who had traveled to Vegas for the weekend but were not fortunate enough to attend the sold-out celebration the night before. Ali's extra appearance reflected his class, love, and heart for people.

As the Champ's entourage accompanied him through the compound, the sporadic low-rumbling chant of "Ali!" "Ali!" "Ali!" could be heard as it resonated throughout the packed casino, hotel, and lobby. Security and a small group of family and staff followed the champion, who rode in a golf cart, slowly descending the red carpet's winding path. They were heading for a professional, regulation-sized boxing ring, specially erected for this event and displayed in the center of the main lobby for the entire weekend. As I watched the Champ roll by me, Ali Jr. stopped and shouted through the cheers, "Where's your gift? Go get the present you brought for my dad!"

191

After hundreds of fans sang "Happy Birthday," two beautiful ring girls, along with Ali's longtime business manager, Gene Kilroy, and former heavyweight champion Evander Holifield, presented my gift to the Champ in the center of the ring amidst a long, rousing ovation.

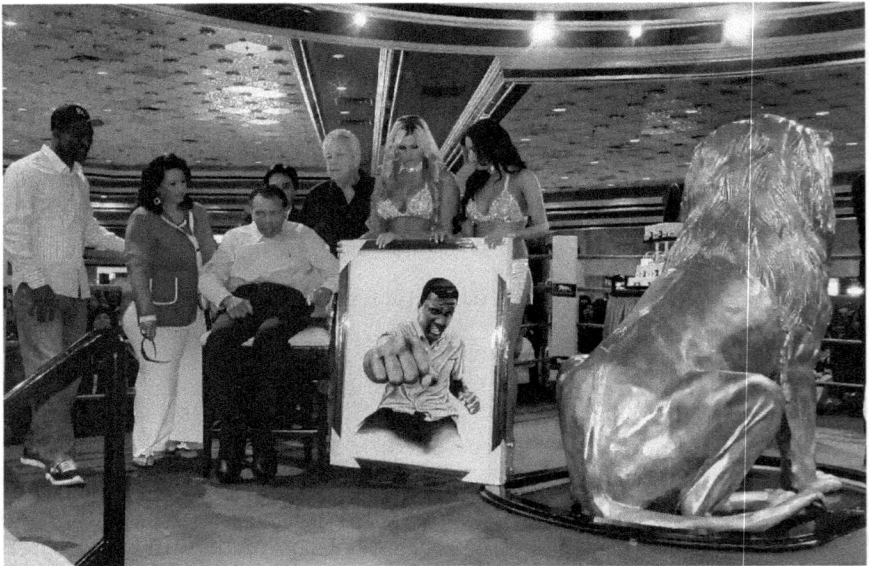

POWER OF LOVE GALA, MGM GRAND HOTEL, SUNDAY, FEB. 19, 2012—*Muhammad Ali receiving my birthday gift—an original black and white oils-on-canvas portrait created by artist Robert L. Stampas, Jr.*

Although my mail correspondence, occasional texts, and phone calls with Ali and his family continued, I didn't know then that this would be the last time I would see "The Greatest" before his death on June 10, 2016. Had I known, I would've included the following letter with my gift.

Dear Champ,

Thanks for the honor of sharing so many precious hours with you. Your extraordinary life was a gift to the world, and I am humbled by the amount of time you graciously spent with me during our cherished friendship. Your presence and wisdom will echo forever in my heart.

The way you lived your life has influenced me and countless others, continuing a legacy that's inspiring new generations! The memories we made together reflect your boundless positive outlook and our unique connection.

Thank you, Champ, for giving me so much of yourself and proving to me that limitless possibilities can come true if we believe, say "Yes!" and act to fulfill our dreams!

DAW

I believe if you keep your faith, you keep your trust, you keep the right attitude, if you're grateful, you'll see God open up new doors.
— JOEL OSTEEN

To receive additional excerpts and other behind-the-scene previews, visit dwayneAwalker.com/previews

INDEX

DECLARATIONS
BY FIVE-D CATEGORIES

INDEX

DECLARATIONS A-Z

-D-

-E-

-F-

-H-

-I-

-L-

-M-

-N-

-O-

-P-

-R-

-S-

-Y-

ABOUT THE AUTHOR

DWAYNE A. WALKER is living proof that all of us can use latent potential to help us create life-experiences and the destiny we desire. At a time in his life and career when he was feeling trapped, Dwayne used the pressures of adversity to discover and unlock talents and gifts, which continue to change and enrich his life today.

Fed up with letting underachievement rob him of the contributions and impact he should make, Dwayne decided to use the simple principle of *sowing*, to begin to *reap* the rich experiences and relationships, he believed God intended for all of us.

Defying logic with how he planted his time, talents, and other resources into the lives of others, he developed unique relationships, including more than a decades-long friendship with the late, great Muhammad Ali.

Dwayne is an author, appeared on national TV, participated in numerous conferences and corporate recognition events across the country, owns an award-winning, ultra-premium, gourmet popcorn enterprise, and is a husband, father, grandfather, and an incredible keynote speaker!

Dwayne encourages individuals to change perspectives, uncover and rediscover abilities, while *inspiring action!* He's dedicated his life to showing others how to unlock and leverage their distinctions to overcome challenges.

INSPIRATIONAL KEYNOTE?

WHEN YOU BOOK DWAYNE TO SPEAK, YOUR NEXT EVENT WILL BE INCREDIBLY
INSPIRATIONAL, THOUGHT-PROVOKING, AND HIGHLY ENJOYABLE!

Dwayne pioneered an effective method of identifying gifts and talents and a systematic approach to leveraging them to drive performance and create personal and professional distinction.

Dwayne masterfully demonstrates how to blend the process of uncovering strengths with the action of using them to achieve desirable and often unexpected results. He turned the distinction of his strong resemblance to Muhammad Ali into a unique relationship with the Champ, which is the basis for his *Becoming a Champion* Keynote Address.

With his high-energy keynote speeches and workshops, Dwayne knows how to engage executives, entrepreneurs, and audiences of all types. He moves organizations and people to a place of contagious clarity and enthusiasm. He can do this for you, too!

Dwayne learned firsthand that you should be yourself in the face of difficulties. Lack of faith and action, makes people afraid to meet challenges. *Believe and take action now!*

To order bulk copies, discuss speaking engagements or consulting programs, please visit dwayneAwalker.com/inquiries.

www.ingramcontent.com/pod-product-compliance
Lightning Source LLC
Chambersburg PA
CBHW052037090426
42739CB00010B/1942